BLACK COUNTRY
Memories 3

Front cover top: *Female workers at Scribbans and Co beside their float for the 'Salute the Soldier' week parade in 1943.* Front cover bottom: *Mitchell's and Butler's Home Guard. (Courtesy of Smethwick Heritage Centre.)* Back cover: *Queen Elizabeth visiting Chance Brothers on 19 April 1940. (Courtesy of Smethwick Heritage Centre.)*

BLACK COUNTRY
Memories 3

CARL CHINN

BREWIN BOOKS

First published by
Brewin Books Ltd, 56 Alcester Road,
Studley, Warwickshire B80 7LG in 2006
www.brewinbooks.com

Reprinted February 2007

ISBN 10: 1 85858 298 9
ISBN 13: 978 1 85858 298 6

A Cataloguing in Publication Record
for this title is available from the British Library.

Typeset in Times
Printed in Great Britain by
Cromwell Press

CONTENTS

ACKNOWLEDGEMENTS

It is a thrill to be writing a local history feature for the *Express and Star*. The paper is not only the biggest-selling evening newspaper in the country outside London, but also it is marked out by its commitment to its region and the people of that region. There can be few papers that are as local as the *Express and Star* and that commitment to localness affects positively every aspect of its reporting and coverage. The Black Country is fortunate to have a paper so dedicated to the well being of Black Country folk. I thank the editor of the *Express and Star*, Adrian Faber, and its management for giving me the opportunity to write so extensively about the Black Country. Adrian has been a constant source of support and encouragement to me and like me is a proud West Midlander. My appreciation is also due to Charlie Brechtman, Adrian's secretary, who carefully and thoughtfully collects all the memories and photos sent in to me; Dave Hotchkiss sub-editor, who puts together my pages in such a talented and sensitive way; and Mark Green, internet information control officer, who has played an important role in sourcing photographs. I also thank the readers of the *Express and Star* who have honoured me by sharing with me their memories and letting me see their photos and precious memorabilia.

FOREWORD

Carl Chinn is a modern day wonder. On the one hand, a serious historian with a vast knowledge of the heritage of the West Midlands. On the other hand, a human whirlwind whose energy and enthusiasm is breathtaking.

His understanding of the West Midlands is second to none. It has been a privilege and a pleasure to have him as part of the Express & Star team. His regular articles are undoubtedly one of the most popular parts of the paper. His legions of fans recognise the depth of knowledge he brings to his subject. He is a writer who has that rare talent of bringing the true human story to the vast breadth of history.

Oddly enough, Carl and myself have followed a similar path in the early part of our lives - growing up in the same part of Birmingham, going to the same secondary school and both attending Birmingham University. Now two Brummies have been reunited in the Black Country.

This is the third of our Black Country Memories books. The first was a sell-out. I shall never forget the queues of people in our front office waiting to tell Carl their stories and have their books signed. It was like a rugby scrum!

I am sure you will enjoy this new volume. It tells the stories of the people and places that have made the Black Country and the West Midlands the great powerhouse of Britain. The articles are sometimes funny and sometimes touching, but never dull.

Carl - thanks, mate.

Adrian Faber

Editor, Express & Star

Black Country Memories

I dedicate this to the people of the Black Country who have kept alive our dialect and whose hard work was vital in making England the greatest manufacturing nation in the world.

Chapter 1

PROGRESSIVE AND MODERN: WOLVERHAMPTON

New Industries were needed desperately across inter-war Britain. The Depression had ravaged the industrial, economic and social landscape of the nation. In particular, it had devastated those areas that were dependent upon the staple industries, such as coal mining, ship building and cotton weaving and spinning. South Wales, Clydeside in Scotland, much of the North West of England, the North East, and West and South Yorkshire were overwhelmed by unemployment – a scourge that afflicted above all adult men who had once earned good and regular earnings. With their loss of work came not only a dire fall in income but also a loss of respect, pride, hope and the status that work gave a man.

The humiliation of being out of collar was exacerbated by the indignity of having to apply for help to the dreaded Means Test, or the Public Assistance. People who had lost their jobs through no fault of their own had to suffer the degradation of the Means Test Man coming in to their homes, assessing their means, and telling them to sell off precious possessions and live off that money before they could be given any assistance.

Novels like *Means-Test Man* (1935) by Walter Brierley drew out the psychological consequences of long-term unemployment. It dwelled upon a week in the life of an out of work Derbyshire miner who lived in dread of the monthly visit of the Means Test Man and it was infused with the author's own experiences – for Brierley himself was unemployed between 1931 and 1935.

Another powerful and thought-provoking novel of the time was Walter Greenwood's *Love on the Dole* (1933), set in Salford, and as well as fictional works bringing to the fore the hopelessness of life without a job there were many investigations and accounts of various forms. These ranged from George Orwell's *The Road Wigan Pier* (1937), in which the journalist related the despair, malnutrition and overcrowding he witnessed in Lancashire and Yorkshire, to Ellen Wilkinson's *The Town That Was Murdered* (1939). In this book the MP for Jarrow wrenched hearts with her account of the Jarrow March of 1936, when 200 men trudged from Tyneside to London to present a petition calling upon the Government to act after unemployment in the town soared to over 70% after Palmer's, the biggest shipbuilder locally, was closed.

All these accounts focused upon the North of England. Others were more wide-ranging. Like the Pilgrim Trust's *Men Without Work* (1938) and *Memoirs of the Unemployed* (1934) edited by H. L. Beales and R. S. Lambert, they drew attention not only to the North but also to South Wales, parts of London, East Anglia, Scotland and the North and East Midlands. But none approached the West Midlands. For all that many parts of the Black Country were as shattered by the Depression as any of the "depressed" areas written about by commentators, they were ignored by commentators.

In 1931 unemployment in the Dudley Employment Exchange Area peaked at 38.8% - although in January of that year it had reached 42.4%. This compared with an average of 22% for Great Britain, 27.4% for Scotland and 33.5% for Wales. A number of other Black Country areas were also badly hit: in Cradley Heath unemployment was 36.3%; in Wednesbury it was 35.7%; in Brierley Hill it was 33.2% and in Bilston it was 31.8%. All of these places were associated with iron and steel and heavy industry – the sectors of industry that had been worst affected by the Depression.

Sadly, unemployment was not much under 30% in Darlaston, West Bromwich, Walsall, Tipton, Stourbridge, Wolverhampton and Walsall. By contrast, the unemployment rate in Oldbury was 23.6% and in Smethwick and Birmingham it was 18.9% and 17.7%. Of course, this was still an unacceptably high figure and behind those statistics lay the reality of tens of thousands of lives in shreds. And it should also be pointed out that in the older, central parts of Birmingham that were dominated by older trades such as button making, brass manufacturing, gun making and jewellery making, the percentage of those out of work was much higher than in outer Birmingham where the new electrical engineering and car factories were based.

Still, Birmingham, Smethwick and Oldbury were places which were not dominated by one major industry, as were Bilston and Brierley Hill, and they were also drawing in the new industries. This was the terrible paradox of the 1930s. Those out of work suffered mentally, physically and emotionally as much as they did economically; whilst those in work benefited from rising real wages at a time when the cost of living was falling along with the size of families. Especially in the South of England where unemployment was generally much lower, these social tends meant that a man in work tended to have more disposable income. This was spent on buying houses, cars and electrical goods – and Smethwick and Birmingham were well placed to adjust to the new demands of the consumers.

It is apparent that the municipal authorities of Wolverhampton were alert to these trends and sought to draw in new industries to the town through the work of the Wolverhampton Industrial Association. This body was made up of aldermen, councillors, the town clerk and development officer, and leading figures such as Geoffrey Mander, MP for Wolverhampton East. The foreword was written by the

Mayor of Wolverhampton, Councillor Bertram Kidson JP. It was an upbeat assessment at a time when Britain, and indeed the world, was in dire economic straits in the aftermath of the Wall Street Crash of 1929. The Mayor emphasised that the trade and population of Wolverhampton was increasing, new factories were opening, house-building was continuing apace, better shopping facilities were appearing, and a general improvement was taking place all round.

Stressing his pride in a municipality that was well-governed, the Mayor added that a new sewage scheme had been completed so that waste could be dealt with adequately, whilst the health of Wulfrunians was "most satisfactory". Indeed, "at no period have the prospects of the town been brighter, and I invite outside manufacturers to establish their new factories in the Borough, confident that they would have no cause to regret their choice". In that last sentence can be discerned, the reason for the publication of a booklet that highlighted the positive attributes of Wolverhampton – the need to attract new industries at a time when old ones were in marked decline.

That reason is reflected on the cover. In the background is the ancient parish church of Saint Peter, but in the foreground is a trolley bus made either by Guy's or Sunbeam and which displays an advert for Goodyear Tyres. It is flanked by a bank and the Queens Cinema and by an Express and Star newspaper seller with a board pronouncing that "Express & Star Wolverhampton Welcomes New Industries".

By 1934 when Wolverhampton brought out the *Industrial and Residential Handbook* a recovery had begun and unemployment locally had fallen from its peak three years earlier to 16.1%. This compared with 21.2% in Dudley, 20.8% in Wednesbury and 18.1% in Walsall. The figures for Oldbury, Smethwick and Birmingham were lower at 11.1%, 9.5% and 8.1% respectively. However, as with all generalised figures we should never forget the large numbers who did not benefit from such a recovery and whose lives were wrecked by continuing high unemployment.

The front cover of the Handbook, *with the Express and Star to the fore.*

How then was Wolverhampton placed to bring in more work? The authors of the *Handbook* explained that "our object in editing and publishing this booklet is to give a truthful and sincere portrayal of life and work in the town of Wolverhampton. In doing so, we have endeavoured to limit the use of superlatives, but if in our enthusiasm we have at times become effusive, we ask forgiveness". It is plain that the reason for the *Handbook* was marketing and although it is not stated, it is as clear that the civic leaders realised that good publicity was essential to sell Wolverhampton to the leaders of industry.

Accordingly, it was reported that "the industrial and commercial importance of Wolverhampton can be attributed to the various factors which must necessarily influence industrialists seeking new centres of activity". These included, raw materials close at hand; well-organised transport by road, rail and canal connecting to the great ports of London, Liverpool, Bristol, Hull and Southampton; a municipal airport in the planning; and a Council that was in good financial health with rates of 11s 6d in the pound. These rates, it was made plain, were much lower than most other industrial towns.

Such positive attributes were enhanced by an energetic and progressive Council that was engaged in clearing "slum" properties and building new houses; by good shops; entertainment "to suit every taste"; beautiful country and picnic spots that were close at hand; a hospitable people; and by "abundant supplies of gas,

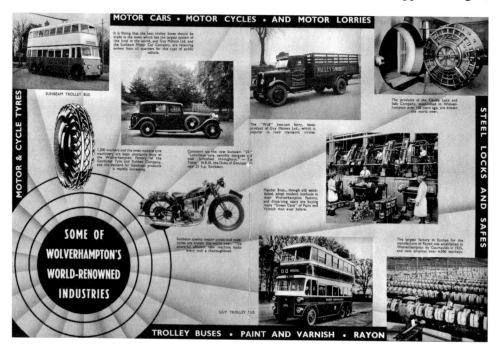

electricity and water available at prices which compare favourably with other industrial areas". As a result "industrialists are showing preference for the town as a location for their new business enterprise".

Amongst those new industrial enterprises that were attracted to Wolverhampton was "the largest Rayon factory in Europe, which now employs 4,000 people". This was owned by Courtauld's, whose main base was on the Foleshill Road in Coventry, and it was opened in 1925. Rayon itself is a man-made fibre that was not synthetic. It is made from wood pulp, a naturally-occurring, cellulose-based raw material. The first knitted garment made entirely from rayon had appeared in 1916 and by the 1930s almost everything in a woman's dress, much of what a man wore and most fabrics had rayon in their manufacture. Thus rayon epitomised the new type of product that was essential if a town was not to become enmired in economic depression.

Another new industry was that of aircraft production. In 1934 Boulton Paul Aircraft Ltd, which had its origins in Norwich, moved to a new factory at Pendeford, just outside Wolverhampton. It brought with it most of the 800 strong workforce and recruited more from Northern Ireland and Scotland. At the same time a training school was set up at Cannock.

The Hawker Demon two seater fighter was the first aircraft built at Pendeford, and as production increased, the factory was extended in 1937. Further enlargements meant that it came to cover three times its original area; whilst the number of employees expanded to 4,800 during the Second World War. During that conflict, the best-known aircraft made by Boulton Paul was the Defiant fighter. Boasting an all metal stressed skin it was powered by a Rolls Royce Merlin 1 engine and was fitted with a Boulton Paul type 'A' turret with four Browning machine guns.

Although it is now too often overlooked, the Defiant played an important part protecting British troops in the evacuation from Dunkirk and in the Battle of Britain in the summer of 1940. Unfortunately, its turret weight made it more cumbersome and after its initial successes there were heavy losses of Defiants that led to it becoming a night fighter.

The Boulton Paul factory itself was an important one and was camouflaged. To add to the deception for enemy bombers, a dummy factory with dummy aircraft was built a mile along the canal in 1940. Fortunately the real factory was never targeted during German bombing raids. Now part of Smith's Aerospace, the Boulton Paul site is a vital one for modern Wolverhampton. It employs highly skilled workers and is geared to the highest specifications of modern technology. That it continues to give so much important work is a testament to the success of Wolverhampton's civic leaders in pulling in new industries in mid and late 1930s.

The *Handbook* brought out by the Council in 1934 was an effective and thoughtful marketing tool. It underlined the progressive nature of the Council and its commitment to carefully-planned and co-ordinated growth. These were important signals. Planning had become of increasing significance since the early twentieth century and any town that wanted to parade its modernistic credentials had to embrace the concept of town planning.

Wolverhampton's officials proclaimed that it was a modern municipality with "broad, well-paved streets, many enhanced by vistas of trees which in Spring and Summer bring the cool countryside into its busy midst. The main thoroughfares of Wolverhampton, lined with first-class shops and offices, offer exceptional merchandising and business facilities. The arcades provided ideal shopping rendezvous in all weathers."

In a sophisticated and clever move, whoever put the Handbook together included an extract from H. V. Morton's *The Call of England* (1928). Educated at King Edward's School, Birmingham, Morton became a journalist on the Birmingham Gazette and Express, rising to assistant editor before moving on to London newspapers. He served in the Warwickshire Yeomanry in the First World War and then returned to journalism, working at the Daily Express from 1921.

Two years later Morton came to prominence with his reporting of the opening of Tutankhamen's tomb. This launched him as one of the paper's most successful columnists. In 1926 he began writing the articles which were later published as *In Search of England*. The book gained Morton a high reputation. His distinctive style intertwined descriptions of his journeys with historical and literary associations. *The Call of England* was a companion to his first successful book.

Both were imbued with Morton's belief in rural England and in the importance of spirituality. As consequence, he felt strongly that industrialisation and urbanisation had harmed the nation. Interestingly, however, Morton was attracted to Wolverhampton. For all that it was a working town that made things, it harked back to a pre-industrial era as much as it reached out to a vigorous, cleaner modern world removed from that of works belching out smoke and pollution. Morton declared that:

There is a quality about certain towns which prints itself on the imagination. Wolverhampton possesses it. Such towns rouse curiosity. They are interesting and complex. They are not sudden industrial mushrooms like many of the big Lancashire manufacturing towns. They were living their busy lives long before there was coal; long before James Watt put the world on wheels. They are market towns of Old England which, because fate planted them near coal and iron, have rolled up their sleeves and entered the New England. Generations of human life, beginning with a shepherd who feared the baying of wolves, and coming down to the daily tramp of the mechanic towards the chimney stacks, give towns like Wolverhampton a strongly defined personality. Such places are alive.

Morton acknowledged that Wulfrunians made "motor cars, safes, locks, keys, and a hundred other things to every part of the world", but for him the town resonated because "the character of an Old English village has been preserved here". It had not lost its rural touch. Proclaiming it to be the capital of the Black Country (an assertion that then surely would have been challenged not only by the people of Dudley but also most Wulfrunians), he went on to praise Tettenhall as one of the two finest suburbs possessed by a manufacturing town. The other was Clifton outside Bristol. With conscious irony he added that "I would much rather live in Tettenhall than in Edgbaston!"

Almost reverently alerting readers to the magnificent Church of Saint Peter, "the greatest treasure of Wolverhampton", Morton's affinity with Wolverhampton was palpable. On a cliff above another church, that of Saint Michael and All Angels, he stood and was transfixed by "the finest view I ever thought to see of the Black Country. To the east lies Cannock Chase; southwards the chimneys of Wolverhampton rise up against the sky, in the evening light reminding one of a great dockyard full of ships; to the south-west lies Sedgley Beacon, Penn and Wombourne; and far on the western horizon is the line of the Clee Hills".

It was a shrewd thing to include Morton's glowing piece in the *Handbook*. The rest of the publication accentuated the Council's desire to portray Wolverhampton as an appealing place in which to set up business, to work, to live, to shop, to be entertained and to enjoy the amenities. There were sections on industry; the low cost of living; road, rail and canal transportation; electricity; water; gas; labour and wages; sewage disposal; the Chamber of Commerce; public buildings; parks and open spaces; health; education; shopping; recreation; and places of beauty around Wolverhampton. The aim was clear: to push forward a clean, progressive, well-planned town with outstanding amenities that was embedded in beautiful countryside and which was linked readily with the outside world.

Crucially, the industries promoted in the Handbook fitted in fully with this positive image. They included Guy Motors and the Sunbeam Motor Car Company, amongst other products

An important centre of the metal industry since the eighteenth century, Wolverhampton's foundries are still thriving, whilst new and lighter industries are being attracted to the town.

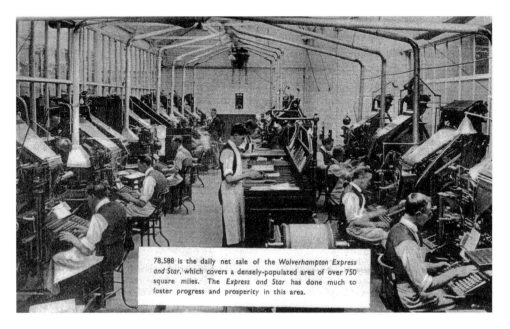

78,588 is the daily net sale of the *Wolverhampton Express and Star*, which covers a densely-populated area of over 750 square miles. The *Express and Star* has done much to foster progress and prosperity in this area.

renowned for their trolley buses; the Goodyear Tyre Factory with its 1,200 workers; the Chubb Lock and Safe Company; Courtauld's Rayon factory; and Mander Brothers which, "though old established, adopts modern methods".

That indeed was the theme of the *Industrial and Residential Handbook*. Though old established Wolverhampton was a modern town which beckoned the future. The authors were not to know that for all the Council's proactive attitude, unemployment in Wolverhampton and across the Black Country and Birmingham was only to disappear with Britain's rearmament from the late 1930s and the onset of war.

I thank Gwen Owen of Wednesfield, who kindly contacted the Express and Star to let me know that she had a book called the Industrial and Residential Handbook that had been published by Wolverhampton Industrial Development Association in 1934. Gwen most generously allowed me to borrow the book and it proved to be a fascinating historical document.

Chapter 2

HILLS AND STONE: ROWLEY

There is an ancient legend that once, when the Anglo Saxons still worshipped the old gods, Thunor bestrode the Clent Hills. Red of hair and beard, and boasting great muscular strength, he was the god of weather and is brought to mind today in Thursday. Readily raised to anger, Thunor was a powerful deity who wielded a mighty hammer and who hurled thunderbolts from mountain peak to mountain peak when he was enraged. The story goes that he fought with his father, Woden, who is recalled in Wednesday, as well as in the Black Country place names of Wednesbury and Wednesfield.

One-eyed, all knowing and draped in his cloak and hood, Woden traipsed across the land when the weather was fine, but when it was stormy he careered across the dark sky at the head of a clamorous wild hunt. During the struggle between the two mighty gods, Thunor is said to have hurled a massive boulder at Woden, who had planted himself upon Turner's Hill in Rowley. The outcome of the terrible fight is lost in the fog of mythology, but Thunor's boulder came to be called Hailstone and so gave another name to Turner's Hill.

Of course, the Anglo Saxons used their tales to explain that which they understood not, but what they did comprehend was the importance of the high ground in the southern marches of the Black Country. Hills dominate the landscape of Rowley and as such they dominate its history. Stand atop Turner's Hill and you are upon a vantage point that at 876 feet is the highest in south Staffordshire and from which there are magnificent views. Nearby are Oakham Hill and Corney Hill. All three hills have been regarded by some as separate peaks of one Rowley Mountain, and by others as an "extensive range of hills terminated by several lofty peaks".

Whatever the case, together these heights form part of the Sedgley-Dudley-Rowley Ridge – a major physical feature that divides England. To the west, rain seeps away to rivers like the Stour that drain to the Bristol Channel and the Atlantic Ocean, whilst to the east that the water feeds into rivers such as the Tame that head towards the Trent and thence the North Sea.

Rowley means the rough clearing, but it is not the clearing itself that has marked the history of the place – rather it is the rocks beneath that clearing that have shaped Rowley. During the course of his investigations for his key work *The Natural History of Staffordshire* (1686) Robert Plot visited Rowley and observed that

A young Tony Crump gazes out towards Portway Farm from its adjacent fields in 1963. This was still a fully working farm with pigs, cattle and horses. Notice the traditional haystack on the left. Thanks to Derek Crump.

scattered here and there all over the town was "a very hard black Shining stone". When polished this "proved a tolerably fair *black Marble*". Still, the stone was difficult to carve "which renders it scarce worth the labour to work it; however, burnt and powdered, it makes very good emery".

However there was one stone locally that was more remarkable than the rest, and it may well be may have been the giant boulder of legend. It lay about a mile north west of the church of Saint Giles and was "as big, and as high, on one side, as many Church Steeples: at the bottom of which on the highest side, if one stamp with ones foot it returns a hollow sound as if there were a *Vault*, which made me suspect that some great person of ancient times might be buryed here, under this *Natural Monument*". Plot went on to suppose that so great a thing could not be put there by art, as it much exceeded the stones of Stonehenge, but digging down he found no evidence of a burial.

From the late eighteenth century, the distinctive stone of Rowley was quarried extensively and it continued to impress those visiting the place. In 1817 in his

Topographical History of Staffordshire, W. Pitt stated that Rowley Mountain had for its base "a singular species of quartzose stone, devoid of any grit quality" that was called Rowley rag-stone. Hard and durable, large quantities of it were "carried to Birmingham and elsewhere, for pavements and repairing roads". A rusty blue in colour, the stone was extremely hard, too much so to be hewn by a common tool, and lay in "an infinite number of fragments, and some of them of immense bulk, both above, upon and beneath the surface".

Fifty years later, J. Beete Jukes in a 'Sketch of the Geological Structure of the South Staffordshire Coalfield' described the striking stone in more detail. He explained that it was basalt, "a black close-grained rock, frequently showing a more or less perfectly columnar structure" that was also found in Powk Hill at Bentley. Each year between 70 and 80,000 tons of

Two Rowley quarry workers. Thanks to Gordon Parsons.

Rowley Rag and other balsatic stone was quarried for road metal, but in the mid-Victorian period it had been hoped that the stone could be used for other purposes, such as making "peculiar forms of glass".

In 1851 a Henry Adcock "conceived the idea of rendering this material available for manufacturing purposes by fusing it and casting it into moulds of the shape required". He noticed that when cooled suddenly after fusion, the basalt was converted into black obsidian, or volcanic glass; but that when it was allowed to cool slowly it resumed its original crystalline basaltic structure, without any apparent difference.

A few experiments showed that the stone could be moulded "without any great difficulty" and Adcock went on to make further experiments in a reverberatory furnace at the works of Chance Brothers. The results were encouraging with respect to two processes. In the first the basalt was fused in crucibles and then cast in red-hot sand moulds, leading to the manufacture of window sills, copings and such like. In the second, the basalt was allowed to cool until it became like plastic, after which

The Rowley and Springfield Despatch Fund for Miners' Kiddies tea at Knowle Methodist Sunday School, about 1913. Mr and Mrs Priest are on the left, and Beatrice Dunn, later Biggs, is on the right. Thanks to Ray Whitehouse.

it was poured onto a metal table and rolled in various thicknesses like rolled glass. The sheets that were formed could be cut with a diamond, again like glass, and were used for roofing or, after polishing, for ornamental purposes.

Patents were taken out and "works were erected on a scale sufficiently large to accommodate what it was then thought would be an extensive department of the glass manufacture. A great variety of articles were manufactured—slabs for steps, window-heads and sills, string-courses, mantel-pieces, doorways, columns and capitals, besides a number of objects suitable for internal decoration, slabs for tables and sideboards, door plates and knobs."

All of these articles "were admirably adapted for the purpose they were intended to serve"; but, unfortunately, production costs were too high to make them competitive. The stone itself was cheap enough, but the great heat required to fuse it necessitated a large expenditure on fuel. This high cost was added to by the need for "the vast variety of moulds required, each demanding the construction of a separate model". Matters were made worse by the extreme intractability of the material after manufacture, and so output was abandoned after three years. The best surviving examples of Rowley Rag glass are in the vestry hall of Edgbaston parish Church, which has columns and ornamental steps cast in the material.

By the middle years of the 1800s, Rowley was described as a straggling parish that was a like a peninsulated promontory of Staffordshire, striking out between detached parts of Worcestershire and Shropshire. Yet it was divided into two manors: Rowley Regis, which was part of the great barony of Dudley and of which Lord Ward was the owner; and Rowley Somery, of which the Duke of Sutherland was lord.

The names of these manors pull us back to the Middle Ages. In the fifty years from 1553 and in a lifetime's work, Samuel Erdeswick surveyed Staffordshire. He indicated that at the Norman Conquest in 1066, Rowley "remained in the king's demesne". This suggests that it was royal property before William the Conqueror defeated King Harold at the Battle of Hastings. In Latin, such ownership was given as 'regis', of the king, and it appears that at various periods the manor was crown land – hence the name Rowley Regis. It is also relevant to note that historically the parish church of Saint Giles was attached to Clent and that the crown was the patron of the living.

Yet it is not clear when the word Regis was added, for the earliest reference to Rowley comes in 1173 when it was referred to as Roelea, whilst a hundred years later the name was given as Ruleye. What is known is that the manor of Rowley Regis was given by King John to a Richard de Rushall and that later it was handed over to the abbots of Halesowen. There are also stories locally that King John had a hunting lodge in Rowley and that he founded the church of Saint Giles. By contrast Rowley Somery emphasised the ownership of the barons of Dudley and recalls a John de Somery who was lord in the early thirteenth century.

Owning the land from which the coal and Rowley rag were dug out, it was the descendants of the medieval lords of the manors who profited the most from the development of industry hereabouts. According to William White's Directory of 1851, Rowley parish comprised "the large but indifferently built village of Rowley, seated on the declivity of a lofty hill, two and a half miles SE of Dudley, and about 20 hamlets". These included Blackheath, Corngreaves, Cradley Heath, Gosty Hill, Haden Cross, Haden Hill, Hayseech, Knoll, Lye Cross, Newtown, Oakum, Old Hill, Portway, Reddal Hill, Slack Hillock, Tipety Green, Tividale, Turner's Hill, Windmill End and Whiteheath. All of them were occupied mostly by nailers and chainmakers as well as miners and forgemen employed in the extensive coal and iron works. Rowley was also a centre for the production of the Jew's (or jaw's) harp, a musical instrument.

Walter White traipsed *All Around the Wrekin* in 1860, describing the onslaught of industrialisation. He remarked how the view from the Rowley Hills "over the region of darkness is singularly striking in contrast with sunshine and verdure". Still, despite the works, mines and factories, Rowley had not yet banished

The buildings at the top of one of the many quarries in the Rowley area in the early twentieth century. Thanks to the Sandwell Community History and Archives Service.

"flourishing hedgerows and wheat fields". The pleasant scenes of the hills, interspersed as they were with quarries, were refreshing to the eyes and the higher White went the more rural it became.

In Rowley Village, "whose church is as conspicuous for miles around as that of Harrow", the "click-click, and thump-thump of hammers in nearly every house" emphasised the prevalence of nailers. The whole village resounded with their strokes and each cottage had its little forge, at which only women worked. Three or four strong, they were sometimes helped by a girl or boy.

The endeavours of the women were an outstanding example of communal action. They shared the fire between them. One after another of the women gave a pull at the bellows, after which each of them "heats the ends of two slender iron rods, withdraws the first, and by a few hammer-strokes fashions and cuts off the nails, thrusts the end into the fire", before moving on to do the same with the second rod. In three hours a woman might make a pound of "fine clout" for which she was paid the meagre sum of thrupence ha'penny – less than 2p in modern money. The women told White that "it ain't work that pays for men and 't ain't much better than clemmin' for women".

Nailers had been prominent in Rowley since at least the 1500s, and their importance is made plain by remarkable statistics from the seventeenth century. In the year from March 1656, 25 weddings were celebrated locally. In nineteen of

Arthur Troman (1st left) and George Knowles with two pals and their dogs outside the Four Ways pub in Portway Road. Arthur spent his working life at Allsop's Hill Quarry. Thanks to Peter Goddard.

them, the bridegrooms were nailers. The fathers of five of the brides also worked at the same trade. Some of these Rowley nailers were substantial farmers, but by the time of White's visit the hand-made nailers were characterised by their poverty. There was little they could do to improve their unhappy condition – even though they tried desperately to do so. In 1842, nailers had gathered in great numbers at Rowley, intending to march on Dudley where many nailmasters lived. Reaching 15,000 in number, the striking nailers were dispersed by troops.

It is likely that male nailers moved into mining, but here again they were faced with hard collar, bad conditions and low pay. In 1827, the Old Lion Colliery was sunk and within a generation there were thirteen pits in Rowley parish. More were to follow, especially in and around Tividale. Unfortunately, too many of the mines were uneconomical – like the Brickhouse Colliery. Sunk in 1824 and covering 66 acres, it was rented by six different coalmasters before it was closed because of flooding in 1881. Two of them were bankrupted by their tenancy.

By this date Rowley Regis was governed by a local board of health (established in 1869), which was entrusted with powers relating to the supply of water, drainage, sewerage, refuse removal and other public health matters. This was superseded in 1894 by Rowley Regis Urban District Council, which was divided into five wards: Cradley Heath, Old Hill, Blackheath, Tividale and Rowley.

Rowley Regis went on to be incorporated as a borough in 1933 and was granted a coat of arms that featured the motto "Loyal and Industrious" and two supporters symbolising local industry. The one is a smith holding a hammer in front of an anvil; and the other is a miner holding a pick that rests on his shoulder and who has a safety lamp around his neck. Both trades have all but gone, along with the nailers and the makers of Jew's harps. Mind you, one quarry remains as a link with the past, whilst the church of Saint Giles also holds out a firm bond with Rowley's history.

Although the modern church dates only from 1923, it takes its name from a saint who is the patron, amongst other things, of woods and poor people. Saint Giles is a fitting choice, for once Rowley would have been a rough clearing in a wood, and for many generations most of its people were poor. They laboured long for little pay and now as we stand as they did on the Rowley Hills and see as they did the impressive views, let us ensure that we hold fast not only to their landscape but also to their memories.

The photos in this chapter are taken from Anthony H. Page, *Rowley Revisited* (Sutton Publishing £12.99). Anthony is another of the few who have brought the history of the Black Country to the many. Raised in Carlyle Road, Blackheath and still a staunch worshipper at the Central Methodist Church, Blackheath, Anthony has striven fruitfully to highlight the past of Blackheath and Rowley, both of which had been under-researched by historians. Energetically, skilfully and selflessly, Anthony has devoted himself to righting this wrong. Reflecting the good-heartedness of the Black Country local historians, Anthony donated the proceeds of his first two books to Saint Giles and Blackheath Central, whilst the proceeds from his third went to Hurst Green Methodist Church, to help a building extension.

Crucially, Anthony has been joined by others such as Tossie Patrick and David Hickman. With her insightful poems that reawaken the Blackheath of old, Tossie has become an inspiration for all of us who seek to arouse the senses when we reach out to the past; whilst David Hickman has diligently and devotedly scoured historical records to widen our knowledge of Rowley, and his thoughtful historical essay is the introduction to Anthony's new book.

David and Anthony are leading figures in the Blackheath and Rowley Local History Society, which began four years back and which has provided a focus for historical enquiry into the area. The Society meets at the Central Methodist Church, High Street, Blackheath at 10.30 a.m. on the third Tuesday of the month, although the next meeting now will be in January. There is car parking at the rear and, as it is a morning meeting, the cafe is open for refreshments, which are included in the entrance charge of £1. Everyone interested in the history of Rowley and Blackheath is welcome.

Rowley Regis is also fortunate in having a superb website dedicated to the district. Rowley Regis Online is a community website that began in 2002 and which aims to provide news relating to Rowley Regis and the surrounding areas and offers members a platform to share their news, views and memories. It achieves its objectives effectively, thoughtfully and successfully. Lively, clear and easy to browse around, it has articles on local history, features on surnames and a section on Haden Hall, amongst others. It can be found at www.rowleyregis.com.

Chapter 3

HISSING OF THE
BLAST FURNACE: BILSTON

Our place names call out to us to hark at what they are telling us. They shout to us to notice those who gave them their names and to understand their meanings. If we do but open our ears we can just catch hold of the men and some women who are recalled in the names of many of our villages, towns and cities. Lady Wulfrun, an Anglo-Saxon noblewoman, who is spoken of countless times a day through the place that she owned, Wolverhampton. The mysterious Dudda, who made a ley, a clearing, in a wooded area in the so-called Dark Ages and who is brought to light each time we say Dudley. And Esni, a leader of his ingas, his people, in the same turbulent time who is quickened whenever we mention Essington.

Beorma of Birmingham, Tibba of Tipton, Aemela of Amblecote, Blocc of Bloxwich, and Secg of Sedgley are amongst the others about whom we know so little but who left us something precious – their names. But it is not only the place names commemorating people that cry to us; so to do those place names that tell us of the landscape of the West Midlands a thousand years ago and more.

From the sixth century, when the Angles and Saxons took over from the Welsh, the new settlers looked well upon the physical features of what is now the West Midlands. Originally following the Black Brook, the River Tame, and the River Stour, they then struck out in family and tribal groups across South Staffordshire, north Warwickshire and north Worcestershire. They did so with fresh and open eyes.

At Walsall they looked down upon a halh, a hollow or small valley, and if you stand today at Saint Matthews that valley is still there below you, despite the generations of building work that has carved away at the terrain. So too remains as conspicuous as ever the hollow in which stands Halesowen. At West Bromwich the Anglo-Saxons saw that broom trees were plentiful and placed a farm, wic, amidst them; whilst at Aldridge it was the alders that grabbed their attention. At Bentley they were impressed by bent grass; whilst at Brierley Hill they fastened upon the briar wood on the hill. And at Bilston they were drawn to a slight rise in the ground that was enough to make it a bill, a ridge.

Bilston was mentioned in 985 in the document whereby King Aethelred gave Wolverhampton to Lady Wulfrun; and again in a charter of 996 when it was written

This eye-catching panoramic view of Bilston brings in both Sedgley Beacon on the far left and the celebrated Elisabeth Furnace on the right. It was taken from the top of Sankey's offices in 1964. In the foreground are some of the old houses that once lined Dudley Street, with Stonefield School just beyond. On the right and edging towards the steelworks is Prosser Street. Thanks to Mike Page.

as Bilsetnatun. This spelling provides us with the full meaning of the name Bilston. As opposed to the old belief that it meant the estate of Bill's folk, it actually indicates the settlement (ton) of the folk (saetan) of the ridge (bill). These people, the Bilsaetan, were noted as early as 860 in a legal document.

The Domesday Book of 1086 stated that at Bilston there was meadow land, a wood about a furlong long and a half broad, and two hides of land. The size of a hide ranged from 60 to 100 acres, depending upon whether the land was good or poor and it was seen as the amount needed for the support of a family and its dependants. Eight villeins and three bordars with their families lived in Bilston, which was worth twenty shillings – the same as Birmingham. Villeins held land but were unfree peasants who were attached to the manor and subject to the lord. Bordars were in the same position but had less land.

Ettingshall was then part of Bilston and had a similar population, but it was worth more; whilst Bradley was smaller and less valuable. Given as Bradelei it meant the broad clearing, but like Bilston, it was destined to thrust off its rural appearance and to become famous as an industrial centre.

Coal was the mineral that powered this transformation. It was dug at Bradley as early as 1315, as was indicated by a grant of land "over against ye cole pitts" made

19

Men at the steelworks about to fill the barrows with coal in 1943. Standing on the steel plates on which the barrows ran and on the left are managers Norman Dean and Frank Hartland. The barrow fillers are Percy Brittle, Tom Burgwin, Henry Maddox and Isaiah Roberts. Thanks to Ken Burgwin.

to Johanna of Wednesbury. As for Bilston, a deed from 1401 made by William Perry of Bilston to his son, John, mentioned property situated near to Windmill Field with two coal pits called the Holloway and the Delves Both are fascinating names. The Delves comes from the Anglo-Saxon word gaedelf, a quarry. Hence the Delves means the diggings – appropriately enough for the getting out of coal. As for Holloway, it relates to a path that had been worn down, hollowed, lower than its original level by the passage of people and animals.

The importance of coal hereabouts was emphasised by Dr Robert Plot in his *Natural History of Staffordshire* of 1686. He explained that a Mr Persehouse of Nether Gornall had stated that at his estate called Moorefields at Moxley "the bed of coal lyes 14 yards thick; inso much that some acres of ground have been sold hereabout for a 100 pound per acre; I was inform'd of one acre sold for 150 pound, and well indeed it might be so, since out of one single shaft there have sometimes been drawn 500 pounds worth of coal." This South Staffordshire coal was vital for the wellbeing of the county, for most of its wood was burned into charcoal for smelting iron in local ironworks and without coal there would have been little fuel for the home.

Coal mining grew in importance over the next century, and as the miners went down deeper so too did the problems of flooding become greater: problems that were partially overcome by the steam engines of James Watt made at the Soho Foundry in Smethwick. By 1825 there 25 distinct coal undertakings in Bilston, although most were small-scale. Seventeen of these collieries produced less than 10,000 tons a year, whilst only that of Scott and Foley fetched out more than 509,000 tons annually.

As late as 1861, 2,000 miners were working in Bilston's collieries, although thereafter the numbers dropped sharply as the small mines closed because of the continuing difficulties caused by flooding and their uneconomic nature. Yet coal was not the only important thing dug from the earth at Bilston. Its grindstones were excellent for edge tools, its sand was much used in the casting of metals, its clay was fired to make bricks, and its valuable iron ore for large castings and such like was to be found above and below the Thick Coal of the ten yard seam. Of these minerals, it was iron that was to make Bilston's name and in that remarkable change the name of John Wilkinson stood out.

A Cumbrian who was the son of an iron founder, "iron-mad" Wilkinson came to Shropshire and South Staffordshire in the 1750s. Some historians think that he built his first coke-fired blast furnace in

Cliff Wilkinson, a brass caster, is pouring molten brass into a mould at the Advance Foundry in Bilston. He lived near to his work in Harrowby Road before moving to Albany Crescent, near to Wolverhampton Street. Cliff was a volunteer Territorial and was one of the first to be called up at the start of the Second World War. A gunner with the Royal Artillery, Cliff was at Dunkirk and managed to board SS Lancastria, which was bombed and sunk. Sadly Cliff was amongst those who were killed. He was just 30. Thanks to the Wilkinson family.

Bradley in 1757, whilst others date it to a decade later. Whatever the year, that first blast of air from a steam pump that blew up the fierce temperatures needed for smelting iron ore was a momentous development; so much so that it has been regarded as beginning the age of iron in Staffordshire, an age that thrust the Black Country on to the world stage as a great manufacturing region.

Although he had important iron works in Shropshire and Wales, Wilkinson's Bradley Works became the cornerstone of his vast undertakings. Castings of all kinds, but especially for steam engines, were produced there and the works were extended in 1772 when additional rolling mills and furnaces were also built. Ten years later, special forges with steam-powered hammers worked by Boulton and Watt engines were set up for the conversion of coke-pig to wrought iron.

Pig iron was impure and an alloy of other elements such as carbon. It was blasted in a furnace and when molten was run into a channel called a runner and from which went right-angled channels known as sows. In turn these led to a set of dead-ended channels called pigs, giving comb-like moulds for the iron. Wrought iron was almost pure and can be hammered and rolled when hot and the developments at Bradley expanded the market.

The upsurge in business meant that the works were enlarged again by 1790, so as to give greater steam power for furnace-blowing, boring, and turning, and for rolling mills and slitting mills. Wilkinson's success energised the whole iron trade locally so that by 1815 there were 55 furnaces at work in South Staffordshire, producing 115,000 tons of pig iron.

Pigeon fancier Bill (William) Walton in his back garden at 6, Pugh Road, Bradley in 1936. Soon after this photo was taken Bill packed up pigeon fancying. The houses in Pugh Road are built from blocks fashioned out of slag from the furnaces of John Wilkinson, the iron master. Today they have been modernized and show no signs of the original blocks. Thanks to Brenda Walton.

A major shareholder in the Iron Bridge project over the Severn River, Wilkinson was magnetised by iron. In 1787, he and his father built the first iron-hulled barrow boat which he floated on the cut at Bradley, where he also paid for the building of an iron pulpit and iron windows in the Methodist chapel. Wilkinson died in 1808 at his house in Bradley and is now recalled by Wilkinson Avenue. He was buried in Cumberland in an iron coffin. Intriguingly, the churchyard both of Saint Leonard's and Saint Mary's C. of E., Bilston hold great iron slabs with a name and date stamped or cast into them. They act as grave markers.

When he died, Wilkinson's Bradley works covered 88 acres. Significantly, he focused his activities upon the Birmingham Canal. Fully opened in 1772, three years after the Wednesbury Old Canal, the Birmingham Canal ended at Aldersley Junction in Wolverhampton. From Birmingham it went through Smethwick, Oldbury and Tipton, whence it made a great loop to bring in Bradley.

Such a diversion emphasised the important of Bilston and Bradley as an industrial centre, an importance that was also made plain in 1818 in Parson and Bradshaw's *Directory of Staffordshire* east of Wolverhampton. This stated that Bilston was principally inhabited by manufacturers of japanned and other wares, colliers and workmen employed in the extensive iron-works. Indeed, "it has been asserted that more iron is made in Bilston-fields than in the whole kingdom of Sweden".

Mr and Mrs Arnold sitting in their living room-cum-kitchen in Tarmac Road in the 1940s. Thanks to Ron Arnold.

Six years later Bilston became a market town by act of Parliament. Wilkinson's works were now owned by Sam Feredey, a coalmaster and banker to boot. They were supposed to be the largest of their kind in the world and deeply affected a contemporary:

The hissing of the blast furnace, the clanging of hammers, the dusky appearance of the workmen, and the various operations upon unwieldy masses of red-hot iron, combine to excite an idea of terror in the spectator:
The ponderous hammer falls,
Loud anvils ring amid the trembling walls:
Strokes follow strokes, the sparkling ingot shines,
Flows the red flag, the lengthening bar refines.
Cold waves immersed, the glowing mass congeal,
And turn to adamant the hissing steel.

Some of the congregation of Ladymoor (Broadlanes) Methodist Church on a Sunday School outing to the Clent Hills, about 1937/38. On the left are unknown, Dora Jones, Gladys Jackson, unknown, Harold France, and Mr Dainty. On the right are Mabel Mullett, Gladys Broadfield, Florrie Humpage, Edna Phillips, Mrs Dainty, Mrs Gough, unknown, Harry Randle, Lucy France, John Kyte and Florrie Cox. Thanks to Gladys Humpage.

Famed for its iron, Bilston was also well known for its tin-plate workers and japanners, those who covered various substances with lacquer. The trade had started in the town early in the eighteenth century and it focused on the lighter and cheaper end of the market and on exports to Spain and South America. Unsurprisingly given the bond between iron and Bilston, most japanned goods from the town were of iron, rather than wood or papier-mâché.

By 1866, japanning employed 400 people, over three-quarters of whom were women and girls. The wages for youngsters were appalling. Boys and girls from eleven to thirteen years old got ls.6d. to 2 shillings (5p) per week at painting; whilst girls of fifteen received 3 shillings (15p). Japanning later declined because of the introduction of electroplating.

The heavy industries of Bilston was a major cause of the Black Country gaining its name, and in 1839 Robson's Directory of Birmingham declared that "the country for miles round is constantly enveloped in one perpetual cloud of smoke". The writer went on to exclaim that:

the roaring of the furnaces, the ear-piercing blast, the clanking of iron chains, and violent agitation of the machinery, the heat of the pavement, and all the innumerable noises incidental to such places, present to the view of the traveller a vivid picture of the poetical descriptions of the infernal regions. At night the country around is lit up by fires, proceeding from the various furnaces, forges, coalpits, coke beds, and lime kilns; while from a hill near this town, towards Sedgley, nearly two hundred blast furnaces, for smelting iron from the ore, may be seen; a sight which probably cannot be obtained in any other part of the world, and in a dark night having an awful appearance.

At this time there were still enamellers in the town. Enamelling had taken hold in the mid-1700s, along with bucklemaking which soon disappeared, however. Through hand painting and later transfer prints, enamelling improved the look and hence the value of metal boxes and other small metal goods then known as toys. This decorative enamelling went into decline from the middle years of the nineteenth century, although the industrial enamelling of iron and steel remained important well into the twentieth century. Fortunately, the art of English enamelling has been revived in recent years in Bilston thanks to Bilston and Battersea Enamels.

The later nineteenth century was a hard time for the folk of Bilston as work dropped off drastically. By 1893 there were just 200 miners locally, 117 of whom, worked at Ladymoor Colliery; whilst japanners and tin platers had all but gone. As for the iron workers, they also had it rough as the mining of iron ore fell and iron works closed.

For too many folk it was work or be clammed and if they could not find collar in their home town then they had to move. Bilston's population peaked at 24,364 in 1861 and thereafter it dropped, not reaching that level again until the twentieth century. The end of the age of iron could have broken Bilston and Bradley. That it did not was due to its doughty people. By dint of the hard work, resolve and ingenuity that they had shown for generations they brought to the fore renowned firms like Hickman's and Stewart and Lloyd's – a story to be told later.

All the photos from this chapter are taken from Ron Davies, *Bilston, Bradley & Ladymoor A Fourth Selection* (Sutton Publishing 2005). Ron is one of a small but mighty band of Black Country chaps who have striven valiantly and successfully to bring the past into the present and to ensure that future generations know that the Black Country was one of the greatest manufacturing regions that the world has seen and that its achievements were founded on the hard graft, skills and determination of its people.

Ron himself is a typical Black Country mon: unassuming, modest, persevering, steadfast, he possesses a dry wit and unflinching dedication to the people of Bilston, Bradley and Ladymoor. This is his fourth book and there is no doubt that our knowledge of Bilston would be the poorer without Ron's achievements. And typical of Ron's generosity of spirit, all royalties from the book will go to the Compton Hospice.

Bilston, Bradley & Ladymoor A Fourth Selection is one of over 55 titles brought out by Sutton after the publishers heeded the appeal made in 1994 by the Black Country Society to extend the *Britain in Old Photographs Series* to the Black Country. The decision has been a resounding success and over 100,000 books have been sold and 14,000 photographs of the Black Country have been brought to a wide audience. I congratulate Stan Hill and the team of seven members of the Black Country Society that met with Sutton's in May 1994 and I pay tribute to the sterling work done by each of the writers.

The Black Country Society was founded in 1967 by enthusiasts led by the late Dr. John Fletcher and it grew out of the Dudley Canal Tunnel Preservation Society which successfully campaigned to save Dudley Canal Tunnel. These pioneers in preserving our history had a hard job. The 1960s was a decade which seemed to turn its back upon our history. Looking forward only, it saw the bulldozing away of much of our history, but spurred on by Dr John Fletcher's boundless enthusiasm, intelligence and commitment and by their own pride in the Black Country, this resolute group stuck to their task. They and those that joined them have made a big difference.

The Society's success are far reaching and long lasting, embracing the emergence of the Black Country Museum, the Black Countryman magazine, its web site, regular meetings, campaigns and books. Details about the Society can be found at www.blackcountrysociety.co.uk or from PO Box 71, Kingswinford, West Midlands, DY6 9YN.

Chapter 4

DELLS AND CHAINS:
OLD HILL AND CRADLEY HEATH

What's in a place name? A lot must be the answer, for the place name to which we belong gives us our local loyalty and makes us hark to the origins of our region. Some Black Country names reach deep into the beginnings of Anglo-Saxon England and even touch the times of the Celts before that - but Old Hill is not one of them. Yet for all that it is a more modern appearance it is an intriguing name, for what does it mean?

Written as Old-hill, this Black Country township of ancient Rowley Regis was shown on Joseph Brown's 1682 Map of Staffordshire, which was included four years later in Robert Plot's invaluable work, *The Natural History of Staffordshire*. Unfortunately, no indication is given as to its origin and even in the monumental Cambridge Dictionary of English-Place Names (2004), Old Hill is not listed. So why is there a puzzle? Surely the name is self-evident and means an old hill. Well there lies the problem, for Old Hill is not on a hill.

A credible explanation for the name was given by J. Wilson Jones, the librarian at Cradley Heath and the author of the *History of the Black Country*. He reckoned that originally the place was Old Dell and that because local people ran the two words together its pronunciation sounded like 'Oldell', and thus became Old Hill. As Ron Moss makes plain in his new book on *Cradley Heath, Old Hill and District* "the name 'Old Dell' appeared to be quite plausible because if you stood on Old Hill Cross, once a staggered crossroads, now a large traffic island, whichever direction you wished to travel in, whether it be 'up to Dudley', 'up to Rowley', 'up to Haden Hill', or even 'up to Cradley Heath' (after crossing a small depression where once there was a ford and where the brook is now culverted under Brook Lane) you had to climb out of a hollow."

However, this apparently reasonable derivation of Old Hill from Old Dell was inaccurate. Instead it seems likely that Old Hill comes from Old Hall, as Ron Moss asserts. In the course of his longstanding and dedicated researches, Ron looked at many old directories in the Salt Library, Stafford. He found several references to addresses that he knew were in Old Hill but which were given as in Old Hall. This led Ron to the conclusion that the Old Hall in question was the nearby Haden Hall.

A superb photo belonging to Mrs J. E. Humphries of workers with oyster 'nets'. Ron Moss has researched chainmaking for over 30 years and there can be no-one living to rival him in his knowledge and understanding of the trade. In the course of his studies, he has photographed chainmakers forging chain and parts for fishing gear for trawlers, but, as he recalls, "I was quite surprised in 2002, when at a lecture, a member of my audience produced two well-worn photographs of her late father and her two aunts who manufactured oyster nets in a forge in Old Field Works, Corngreaves, Cradley Heath." This particular picture shows Joseph Morris and his two sisters with the oyster net they have just made in front of them.

The Haden family had owned land locally from soon after the Norman Conquest, for in the later eleventh century a Ricardo atte Haudene was given permission to build a dwelling on a hill in Rowley. This became known as Haden Hill. In the later Tudor period a bigger and grander structure was constructed on the site. Called Haden Hall it is still there.

This building was inherited by George Alfred Haden Haden-Best in 1877. Born in 1839 he was the son of Emiline and Benjamin Best. Emiline herself was the daughter of Mary Kendrick and the redoubtable and intimidating Reverend George Barrs. It was Mary's second marriage, for she was the widow of John Haden and it was through this connection that Haden Hall was passed down to the Bests.

Unhappily, George Best was not keen on this old building as the home of a Victorian gentleman, and so, just a year after he came into its possession he had built Haden Hill House in front of Haden Hall. He had intended to knock down the Hall, but his old aunt lived there until 1903. By then the ageing Best had lost the will to become involved in any more construction work and thankfully the Hall escaped demolition.

The park that enclosed the buildings was landscaped by Best and he lived at Haden Hill House with his two adopted daughters until he died in 1921. The next year, a three-day sale of the contents of the house was held, but the house and estate were saved for the local people by a committee that was determined to raise the purchase price from businesses and other folk. When this was achieved, the house and grounds were presented on 21 October 1922 to the then Rowley Regis Urban District Council, for the enjoyment of the public in perpetuity.

In his book, Ron Moss reveals that the Council actually proposed to demolish the Hall in 1934 because its position was becoming dangerous. Joseph Perry and his

A cracking view of celebrations at the coronation of King George VI and Queen Elizabeth (the late Queen Mother) in Best Street, Old Hill from the Collection of the late Mrs Dorothy Andrews of Dudley Wood Road. Ron Moss has included a number of photos from this smashing collection in his new book on Cradley Heath, Old Hill and District. They were probably taken with a family-owned Brownie box camera. Best Street brings to mind George Alfred Haden Haden Best.

brother, the Reverend Lyttleton Perry, had been involved in the original campaign to save the buildings and they sprang back into action against the new threat. Again they called for help from local businessmen, including from Mr A.M. Bassano, a nephew of George Alfred Haden Haden-Best. Happily they raised the funds for the necessary repairs. Joseph Perry himself made chain in Lawrence Lane, Old Hill and as an avid reader was often seen with a book whilst making chain. He was also a lay preacher who wrote many poems and was dubbed the Chainmaker Poet.

During the Second World War, Haden Hill House was used for issuing ration books, a Ministry of Food store was maintained there, and overnight accommodation in the library was given to local families who had been bombed out. In the post-war years, the house once more fell into disrepair and local people had to fight hard yet again to stop the destruction and disappearance of the two historic buildings. These community activists founded the Haden Hill Preservation Society and the Haden Hill Park Protection Trust. They were successful in their campaign and after several years restoration work, Haden Hill House was reopened for the public in 1989.

Today the Grade 2 listed Haden Hill House is furnished as it would have been between 1878 and 1921, when it was Mr Best's home. It boasts conference facilities, is licensed for Civil Marriages, and is available for evening talks and tours

Cradley Heath Salvation Army Band returning to their barracks in Newtown Lane via School Street after the members had played for the Saint Luke's School 'treat and parade' about 1931. The school, in the background, is still in regular use. This is a photograph supplied by Ron Griffiths.

A chara outing, probably from the Bible Class of the Macefields Mission, Old Hill, about 1920 and from the Collection of Ms J. Walker. This charabanc was bought by Samuel Johnson, 'Supreme' Limited, of Stourbridge in 1920. Samuel was born in 1879 in King Street, Old Hill. Ms Jennifer Walker who loaned Ron Moss the photo states that her step-grandfather is the chap in the dark overcoat and trilby hat above the word 'Stourbridge'.

for local societies. Guided tours can be booked as can school visits. There are also exciting plans to restore Haden Hall.

Down the hill from the hall, Old Hill developed as a distinctive place, although in *F. R. Melville's Directory of Dudley and District* of 1852 it was placed under the heading of Halesowen. That publication had only three references to Old Hill. The first related to Henry Holloway, a manufacturer of wrought nails, rivets, tenter hooks, cable and trace chains, and a dealer in anvils, vice hammers, and wrought-iron gas tubes. The second mentioned The Cross at Old Hill, from which letters were despatched; and the third was an advertisement for W. H. Nock of the Four Ways Family Brewery, 'Cradley Heath near Old Hill'.

Thirteen years later, *Jones's Mercantile Directory of the Iron District* correctly placed Old Hill with Cradley Heath as part of Rowley Regis. It revealed that Old Hill had a postmaster; a Primitive Methodist Chapel; a variety of shopkeepers; several pubs; and plenty of industry. There was a tube works; the blue and red brick and tile works of Partridge Guest and Kaybould; three coalmasters, one of which ran the Ash Tree Collieries and another the Old Hill Colliery; several small-scale chainmakers; and the Waterfall Works of Noah Hingley, where chain and trace was made. Timothy Hingley also made nails at this works, which gave its name to Waterfall Lane. This was the only place given as a separate address within Old Hill.

At the turn of the twentieth century, Old Hill's population had reached 10,798, according to *The Black Country and its Industries* (1902 and 1905). This was 3,000 more than that of Cradley, and almost 1,800 more than that of Cradley Heath. Chain making was the most notable trade in Old Hill, but the name of H. W. Shaw was also well known as an iron manufactory. Here was produced not only a variety of chain but also ship tackle and forgings, nails, rivets, bolts, horse shoes, spades and shovels, and gasfitters' and plumbers' tools and irons. Then there was James Billingham, who had a large boot factory, employing over 100 people; and Willetts the builders, responsible for the construction of the Wesleyan Chapel and School on the Halesowen Road, Old Hill.

This swelled the number of chapels locally. The 'Prims', Primitive Methodists boasted places of worship on the High Street, at Gorsty Hill and on Reddall Hill. Then there was Macefields Mission in Claremont Street; the Ebenezer Strict Baptists in Station Road; the Particular Baptists in Spring Meadow; the Zion Hill United Methodist Church and also the Salvation Army on the Halesowen Road;

Ron himself took this photo of High Street, Cradley Heath on 16 May 1959. The Midland Red bus 244 has almost finished its journey from Wednesbury to Cradley Heath via Great Bridge and Dudley. Many of the buildings in the shot are still there.

Another photo by Ron Moss of the floods in Old Hill. In both 1968 and 1969, heavy downfalls of rain caused floods locally, so that only heavy buses and lorries could get along the Halesowen Road. The bus in view is a Midland Red number 243. Much of the property on the right has been demolished.

and the Saint James's Wesleyan Reform Church on the Cross. Finally there was Holy Trinity Church of England.

With its Grand Theatre on the Halesowen Road, Old Hill was a self-sufficient town. Its people and its determined band of independent retailers ensure that it remains a place of distinction, as does Cradley Heath. Separated from Cradley, once in Worcestershire, by the River Stour, Cradley Heath was in Rowley Regis and thus Staffordshire.

Cradley itself was mentioned as Cradelei in the Domesday Book of 1086 and means the wood or clearing of a man called Cradda, or else the cradle clearing, that is the clearing where cradles or hurdles were made. Thus although separated by a river, Cradley Heath would be the heather land of Cradley – although this name seems to have emerged much later. Cradley Heath was not shown on Browne's Map of 1682, although a place called Forge is indicated close to the position of the later Cradley Heath, just to the south of Old Hill and on the Stour, across from Cradley.

Both Emmanuel Bowen's Map of 1749 and J. Harrison's Map of 1788 also showed Forge in this position. Confusingly, on William Yates's Map of 1778,

Cradley Forge is showed south of the Stour. This map also shows Cradley Heath for the first time. What is certain is that Cradley did boast forges that had been owned by Dud Dudley, the ingenious illegitimate son of the Baron of Dudley. These works were destroyed by floods in 1623, although later in the century the Cradley Forge and Mill were operated by John Wheeler.

Interestingly there is also mention of Corngreaves Forge in the eighteenth century. This was in what would become Cradley Heath. In 1834 William White noted in his *History, Gazetteer and Directory of Staffordshire* the extensive iron and steel works of the New British Iron Company at the Corngreaves, which gave its name to Corngreaves Road. Twenty-four years later the company gained an agreement to mine under the Haden Hall Estate, but only from pits and shafts outside the property. For this the then owner, Frederic Barrs, received the huge sum of £50,000. The deal must have been helped by the fact that the agent of the New British Iron Company had been Benjamin Best. He had died four years before but had been the brother-in-law of Frederic and was the father of George, who inherited the Haden Hall Estate.

The 'Corngreaves Hotel' at the corner of Graingers Lane and Corngreaves Road, Cradley Heath, about 1900. Thanks to the collection of Peter Barnsley. This pub was run for many years by the Cole family, who also ran a saddle and harness maker's from the premises.

White's Directory also indicates that Noah Hingley, later so closely associated with Netherton, was still involved in making nails in Cradley Heath, as he had been for many years – although he had long since moved into the manufacturing of anchors as well.

Within a few years, Cradley Heath had become a significant town. It had its own gas company, police station and working men's club, as well as two Primitive Methodist Chapels, a Baptist Chapel and Saint Luke's Church of England, Reddall Hill. Like Old Hill, Cradley Heath was renowned for its chainmakers, many of whom were to be found in the Lomey Town locality, but it also had a wide range of other manufacturers. These included Henry Barnsley, a Jew's harp maker; Joseph Barnsley who was a welded wrought iron tube maker; and Thomas Barnsley of the 'Cross Gun's' pub, who was also a gun barrel maker. A number of other men doubled up in their jobs, amongst them George Dudley of Whitehall, who was a farmer and coalmaster.

At the turn of the twentieth century, Cradley Heath's name was being taken around the world through its products belonging to firms such as E. S. Bloomer and Co., general engineers; Albert Jackson, fishing tackle manufacturers; C. Harris, anchor makers; and Joseph Penn's iron rolling mills at the Providence Iron Works. Still, it was as the headquarters of the world's chainmaking and cable industry that the town found fame, with businesses such as Richard Sykes and Son, Richard Green, George Allen, S. Woodall, Mark Attwood, J. Gilbert, Samuel Woodhouse, S. Tromans and Sons, Gideon Billingham, and J. B. Homer and Son.

A town of vitality, Cradley Heath had a thriving market, its own building society and was the centre of both the Chain Manufacturers' Association for the employers and the Chainmakers' and Strikers' Association and the Block Chainmakers' Association for the workers. With a picture house in Foxhall Street and another in Lomey Town and with the Empire Theatre of Varieties on the High Street, Cradley Heath was also a focal point for entertainment. And if those were not enough, the town also claimed an orchestral society, a male voice choir and a prize band for the musically minded - and for the sportingly inclined it had two football teams, the Early Closers and Saint Luke's; a bowling club; a tennis club; and a tennis and hockey club.

Cradley Heath was a remarkable place. Small both in area and population, it thrust itself on to the world stage through the endeavours of its people, and those people exemplified the way in which a town can become a community not only through the shared experiences of work but also through the collective experiences of membership in clubs and associations.

The photographs in this chapter are taken from Ron Moss, *Cradley Heath, Old Hill and District. A Second Selection*, (Sutton Publishing, £11.99). It is one of over 55 titles brought out by Sutton after the publishers heeded the appeal made in 1994 by the Black Country Society to extend the *Britain in Old Photographs Series* to the Black Country. The decision has been a resounding success and over 100,000 books have been sold and 14,000 photographs of the Black Country have been brought to a wide audience. I congratulate Stan Hill and the team of seven members of the Black Country Society that met with Sutton's in May 1994 and I pay tribute to the sterling work done by each of the writers.

Ron Moss himself is an extraordinary man, who is imbued with a determination to keep alive the history of the Black Country and its people. The author of several books, he is chairman of the Industrial Group of the Black Country Society, a key figure in the preserved chainshop at Mushroom Green and an advisor for the Black Country Living Museum. Indeed Ron has written the definitive book on chainmaking. It is called *Chainmaking in the Black Country* (Blakemore Publications).

Chapter 5

GREEN AND BLACK: HALESOWEN

So many of our place names are derived from words that were used by the Anglo-Saxons to describe the landscape in which they settled and which they had taken over from the Welsh. Dudley is one of a number that finish with the word leah, transformed into ley and meaning a woodland clearing – in this case of a man called Dudda. It probably emerged sometime between about 750 AD and about 950 AD, a couple of hundred years after the Anglo-Saxons had conquered what is now the west midlands. Several other place names came about in the same period. Amongst them are Bentley, signifying the clearing of bent grass; Rowley, the rough clearing; Langley, the long clearing; and Cradley, the clearing of man called Cradda or else the clearing where cradles or hurdles were made.

The New Hawne Colliery about 1912. (Dudley Libraries)

Across the Black Country there are also a marked number of place names ending in "al" or "all", from the Anglo Saxon word halh. This meant nook and was related to holh, a hollow. Usually, halh refers to a sunken place or recess, but sometimes it could be used to describe a nook of land between rivers, or for slightly raised land in a marsh. However, in the west midlands it is as a shallow valley that the term halh was most used.

Today it is often difficult or indeed impossible to make out such a nook, because urbanisation and development have too often destroyed or obscured the original lay of the land. Exceptions are Shifnal in Shropshire, which can still be seen in a large, shallow basin – in this case having belonged to man named Scuffa; and Bednall in Staffordshire, the nook of Beda. Walsall indicates the nook of Walh, itself either a man's name or inferring the survival of a Welsh presence. Although its parish church, Saint Matthew's, lies upon a limestone hill in the centre of the modern town, the ground falls away on all sides and there is a noticeable dip in the Bridge Street area, where the Walsall Brook flowed.

Elsewhere in the Borough of Walsall, lie Pelsall, Peol's nook; Rushall, the nook with rushes in it; Willenhall, the nook of a chap called Willa; and Blakenhall, which may mean Blaca's nook or else the settlement at the black nook. Further south lies Halesowen, which for many years was simply Hales – the nooks. Certainly, coming down Mucklow Hill, Halesowen as a town does lie in a pronounced dip, but as with Walsall, its parish church of Saint John rises from higher ground.

The plural Hales suggests that there were nooks elsewhere locally, although much of the old manor of Hales was upland – as with the hamlets of Quinton (Ridgeacre) and Hill. Given as Hala in the Domesday Book of 1086, Halesowen had a home farm belonging directly to the lord, which boasted four ploughs, and another estate where Roger the Huntsman had six tenant farmers and five smallholders. In addition, the main part of the manor had 66 men of various social and economic standing and two bondswomen. If we take into account the

The 'Old Lyttleton Arms', High Street, about 1910.

families of the men, then Halesowen may have had a population of around 400 – ten times that of the poor manor of Birmingham.

Importantly, the Domesday Book also recorded that Halesowen had two priests. Given that there were 57 parishes in Worcestershire with 60 priests, it is noteworthy that the settlement was one of only three in the county with a pair of priests, suggesting that the local church was a significant one. The priests were appointed by Roger of Montgomery, a powerful magnate who was a close friend and adviser to William the Conqueror, the Norman leader who had violently taken control of England from the Anglo Saxons. Roger's main base was Shrewsbury, from which he was encharged with protecting the Marches from the Welsh. Because of this association, Roger parted Halesowen from Worcestershire and made it a detached portion of Shropshire, where it remained until 1844 when it was returned at last to its original affiliation.

The manor of Halesowen itself was a wide one, although it no longer included Cradley, Lutley and Warley Wigorn (that part of Warley in Worcestershire) as once it had done. For all that, it embraced a large number of hamlets. These were Romsley, Hunnington, Illey, Lapal, Hasbury, Hawne, Hill, Cakemore, Ridgeacre (Quinton), Oldbury and Warley Salop, the portion in Shropshire. All of these were passed on to Roger's second son, Hugh. He was killed in 1098 in a battle with a raiding party of Vikings in Anglesey, and was succeeded by his older brother, Robert de Belleme. It was he who lost Halesowen after he joined a rebellion against Henry I that failed.

Like the rest of Robert's lands, Halesowen became the property of the king, hence the emergence in the twelfth century of the name Hales Regis. Under Henry II, the manor was then given to his sister, Emma. She was married to Dafydd ap Owain, the son of Owen the ruler of the North Welsh kingdom of Gwynedd. As a result Hales Regis became Hales Owen – and this was the name that was to take hold and become long-lasting.

For a short time David himself became king of Gwynedd, but he was soon replaced. He died in 1204 so that Halesowen went back to King John. Ten years later he gave it to Peter des Roches, the Bishop of Winchester, "to build there a house of religion of whatever order he chooses". Peter decided to put up an abbey for the Premonstratensian order of monks. Known as the 'White Canons", they became the dominant force in Halesowen until the Reformation when Henry VIII dissolved all religious houses.

A year later, in 1539, the king sold the manor of Halesowen to John Dudley, who had come into ownership of Dudley Castle recently. An ambitious soldier turned statesman, Dudley rose rapidly, gaining the grand titles of the Earl of Warwick and the Duke of Northumberland. During the reign of the sickly Edward VI, he became the virtual ruler of England. A keen Protestant who was keen to keep the monastic lands he had bought so cheaply, Dudley feared that Edward would be succeeded by his older sister Mary. She was a resolute Catholic and might restore the monastic lands.

When the king died, the overweening nobleman sought to maintain his authority by placing his daughter-in-law, Lady Jane Grey, on the throne. His move failed. Lady Jane Grey and her husband were executed. Dudley tried to save himself by renouncing his faith, declaring that "A living dog is better than a dead lion". His unfaithfulness could not save him and he was also executed.

Legally, a traitor's lands reverted to the Crown, but Halesowen had been settled on Dudley's wife, Joan, in 1539. She managed to hang on to the manor and it went to her sons. One of them, Robert, became a favourite of Queen Elizabeth. The Earl of Leicester, he was a notorious figure who was suspected of poisoning his first wife, and who later had a bigamous marriage. He decided to hold on to the township of Oldbury but sell Halesowen. It was bought by two local men who made their money by selling the best farms to their sittings tenants on 1,000 year leases. In 1558, what was left of the manor of Halesowen was bought by Sir John Lyttleton, whose main estate was nearby at Frankley and who also owned Arley, near to Bewdley.

A staunch Catholic, Sir John also purchased the manors of Cradley and Hagley. Once again, Halesowen was to be embroiled in the twists and turns of high politics and religious controversy. Sir John himself managed to be accepted at court, but his grandson, another John, was less fortunate. He inherited his family's lands in 1599 and was implicated in the attempts of the Earl of Essex to raise a rebellion against Queen Elizabeth. The stepson of Robert Dudley, the former lord of Halesowen, Essex was handsome, brave and foolhardy and was beheaded for his treason.

As for John Lyttleton, his life was spared but he died in prison in 1601. Once again, Halesowen went back to the Crown. Four years later, Lyttleton's cousin, Stephen Lyttleton of Holbeach, near Stourbridge, was hung, drawn and quartered for his involvement in the Gunpowder Plot; whilst his brother, Humphrey, was executed for aiding and abetting the plotters.

And yet again, a widow was able to regain Halesowen for her family. Meriel, the wife of the unhappy John, had the manor restored to her on condition that she brought up her sons as Anglicans. It was she who made Hagley Hall the family base. A stubbornly Royalist family in the English Civil War, the Lyttletons managed to keep their estates. During the eighteenth and nineteenth centuries, the family sold many of its farms and business premises but continued to take an active in the political and economic life of the area. The title of Viscount Cobham was inherited in 1889, but the Lyttletons have also held on to the title of lord of the manor of Halesowen.

In the past, one of the major sources of income for the Lyttletons was the iron furnace at Halesowen. Iron working was long-established in the locality. In 1312 the

Halesowen from Church Lane (Dudley Libraries).

Abbot of Hales gave permission to a Richard Faber "to found and build a forge near the bank of Haymill, and to raise tin from which he may forge hatchets and other arms for the term of his life". In his deeply informed book on the History of Halesowen, Julian Hunt (Phillimore 2005), states that this forge would have been on the River Stour and that it would have had a water wheel to power its forge hammer. He goes on to propose that it may have been sited at the bottom of Mucklow Hill, where the place name Haywood is to be found, or else at Hayseech, where the Stour forms the boundary with Rowley Regis.

Over the ensuing centuries, more forges appeared on the Stour and in the early 1600s the Lyttletons themselves set up a blast furnace at the foot of Furnace Hill, close to the bridge over the River Stour and across which went the old Halesowen to Dudley Road. By 1642, this was leased by Richard Foley. His family maintained control of it in their own right and through various partnerships until the early eighteenth century. Then in new hands, the Halesowen Furnace carried on as a vital facility. In 1757-8, it produced 821 tons of pig iron, but thereafter it declined. A charcoal-fired furnace, it lost out to competition from the new furnaces that used coke for smelting iron and it closed down in 1772.

Julian Hunt also reveals that a malt mill at the bottom of Mucklow Hill was turned into forge in the mid-1700s, and that between 1900 and the 1960s this site was run by John Brown and Sons, manufacturers of spades, shovels and forks. There was also a slitting mill nearby. Here the iron produced in the forges and furnaces of the Stour Valley was slit, cut into smaller pieces, so that it could be sold to nailers.

The hundreds of men and women who actually made the nails laboured long and hard for little reward. It was the wholesalers who profited from the trade. Emerging from the ranks of farmers and minor gentry and with capital and property already behind them, these men were an elect band that bought the finished nails as cheaply as possible and then sold them on. Amongst the most successful were the Bissells, originally of Webbs' Green Farm, and the Greens of Greenhill Farm, Mucklow Hill.

This locality was the favoured spot of Walter Somers. In 1866 he set up a small ironworks that came to specialise in heavy forgings for ships and steam engines. Business prospered and by 1884, Walter was able to buy a seven-ton Nasmyth hammer. Within twenty years this had been superseded by a 3,600 ton hydraulic press that cost the great sum of £8,500. The Somers family are recalled in the Somers Sports and Social Club, and the firm of Somers Forges continues to ensure that manufacturing remains important in Halesowen. James Grove and Son also maintains the link with the town's manufacturing heritage. Founded in 1857 as a button factory it continues to make quality products.

Another important industry locally was that of making gun barrels and tubing. During the eighteenth century several corn mills on the Stour were converted into forges or gun barrel boring mills. One such was Hayseech Mill, associated with the Buss family from 1801 until, the 1860s, and then operated by the Birmingham Gun Barrel Company. A slightly later concern was that of the Roses. In 1848 they took over

A shortcut through the churchyard of Halesowen Parish Church in 1975.

the gun barrel manufactory which had been the Halesowen Slitting Mill. Within a few years, the family had moved into rolling tubes for the growing gas and water industries. Later they formed the National Tube Company and moved to a new factory on the corner of Prospect Road and Mucklow Hill. Their old premises were taken over by the Halesowen Steel Company Limited.

The biggest factory of all in the making tubes was that of Stewarts and Lloyds. Arising from a business founded by Abraham Barnsley, it was located on the east side of the Dudley Canal at Coombs Wood. After Stewarts and Lloyds emerged in 1903, the factory expanded across the canal and came to cover 56

The Market Cross at Halesowen in 1961.

acres. In the Second World War, the company designed and installed PLUTO, the Pipeline Under The Ocean, that facility that was so vital to the success of the Normandy landings because it took oil under the English Channel to the Allied troops in France and allowed them to advance against the enemy.

Of course, Coombs Wood was as well known for its colliery developed in the early twentieth century – although coal had been dug here since the later Middle Ages. In 1281, the Halesowen Manor Rolls mentioned that five loads of sea coal were raised locally, and in 1307, the Abbot of Halesowen leased a coalmine in the manor to Henry Hill. He was allowed to open two pits and to employ four picks in each. For many years, coal outcropped on Mucklows Hill and was worked by quarries and then shallow shafts, but it was not until the nineteenth century that coalmining developed fully in Halesowen. Amongst the most important pits was New Hawne Colliery, where the sinking of shafts began in 1865 and which supplied coal to the Corngreaves Ironworks and Furnaces in Cradley Heath. It closed in 1921.

A town noted for its industries, yet Halesowen was embedded within a decidedly rural hinterland and was on the western and green edges of the Black Country. It was also a market town from the early thirteenth century, a shopping centre for its district and, for a while, it was an important place in the canal system – for the Dudley Number 2 Canal runs through Halesowen and connects with the Worcester and Birmingham Canal at Selly Oak.

Although growing in the 1800s, Halesowen was reduced in size that century by decisions taken by national governments. Oldbury and both parts of Warley, Wigorn and Salop, were detached, whilst Romsley and Hunnington were given to Bromsgrove. From 1894, the Halesowen Rural District Council governed what was left of the old manor of Halesowen along with Cradley, as well as The Lye and Wollescote until 1897. Quinton was then lost in 1910.

In 1924, the authority became an Urban District Council and borough status followed in 1936. That independence was lost in 1974 when Halesowen and Cradley became part of the Borough of Dudley. By then many of Halesowen's historic buildings were falling before the onslaught of concrete, steel and glass so beloved by designers of modernistic and utilitarian structures. Old Halesowen disappeared from great swathes of the townscape, and the place was refashioned as comprehensively as major cities such as Birmingham and Coventry.

Still old Halesowen does call out to us here and there to hark to its past. It calls out in Saint John's Church, with its Norman features; in the ruins of Halesowen Abbey; in the Dudley Number 2 Canal; in businesses like that of James Groves; and in the Leasowes, the magnificent park where Shenstone the Poet pioneered the natural landscaping of gardens. Now part of the urbanised West Midlands, Halesowen remains a proud and distinctive town.

Chapter 6

BLACK COUNTRY BRAVERY: THE BOER WAR

The Boer War (1899-1902) caught hold of the emotions of the British public in a way that no other colonial war had done before. Perhaps it was because the war broke out as the long and glorious reign of Victoria was about to be dowted, just two years after the spectacular celebrations to acclaim her diamond jubilee. Perhaps it was because the early successes of the smaller Boer forces shattered the self confidence of Britain as the world's foremost economic and imperial power. Perhaps it was because popular newspapers sent out special war correspondents to South Africa and were able to daily despatch their reports back home to feed the thirst for news of an increasingly literate public. And perhaps it was because of all of these factors.

Whatever the case, the Boer War involved the public at home in a way that no war had before and the successes and failures of the British armies became indicators not only on the present state of the nation but also of its future condition.

Descendants of Dutch and French Huguenots (Protestant) who had settled from the seventeenth century in what became South Africa, the Boers were a hardy and independent-minded people who came to believe that they were a people chosen by God. After Britain had taken over the Cape Colony from the Dutch in 1795, many of the Boers chaffed at the political and legal control of what they perceived as an alien power that had no wish to understand either them or their ways.

Looking down on Black people as inferior, they were dismayed that Britain passed an act to free slaves in 1833. Determined to throw off British rule and to protect their racial superiority, large number of Boer families headed off into the interior to be free of British interference, and, as one of them put it, to "preserve our doctrines in purity". This Great Trek as it was called may have been a freedom march for the Boers but it meant subjugation for many Bantu tribes. After bloody battles, both the Matabele and the Zulus were defeated and the Boers sought to set up a state in Natal. The British would not countenance it, because the province had a coastline important to the passage of British ships around the Cape and towards India.

The Boers hitched up their wagons again to escape the long shadow of the British. Outnumbered by the Bantus, yet because they had the firepower of guns they took over the lands between the Orange and Vaal Rivers. When the British led by Sir Harry Smith, whose wife was recalled in Ladysmith, took over this wide area, some Boers went across the Vaal River into the Transvaal, where based on large extended family groups they formed a loose confederation.

The British decided to let them be. Independence was ceded to the Orange Free State and the Transvaal, the constitution of which was based on the inequality of Blacks with Whites. Yet British policy was fickle and in 1877, the British flag was raised in Pretoria, the capital of the Transvaal, by Rider Haggard – who went on to find fame as a writer of King Solomon's Mines and other books.

Just over three years later, the Boers rose up and after defeating a British detachment at Majuba Hill they secured their independence. The discovery of gold

Elsie Lee of Bloxwich was prompted to write to me by the discussion in the Express and Star about a supposed memorial to local Boer War veterans in Wednesbury. Herself one of the last women chainmakers of the Black Country, Elsie told me that her father was one of the first volunteers for the Boer War and she kindly enclosed a picture of the first batch who went out to South Africa. Her father, Ralph Smith is on it, second from the right. He was only nineteen and his name is on the plaque in Walsall Town Hall.

With all the talk over the last year about the Second World War, and also the First World War, it got Elsie wondering about her dad's service. She recalls that as a youngster she heard "scraps of the war between him and my mother", but not much more than that. Elsie thinks that her father enlisted with his future brother-in-law. Her mother's brother was called Tom Astbury and he was sadly killed. Ralph himself went on to serve fourteen years in the Army and died in 1941.

in the Transvaal in 1886 ensured that this was short-lived. British miners and prospectors, called Outlanders, poured into the Boer states and especially to the huge new town of Johannesburg. Surrounded by British colonies and protectorates, the Boers began to fear that they would be overwhelmed from within; whilst the Outlanders called out that they were heavily taxed yet excluded from government.

Joseph Chamberlain, the charismatic MP from Birmingham who was Colonial Secretary, threatened force if the Boers did not address the grievances of the Outlanders. The Boers backed down, but not for long. A newly united Germany led by a Kaiser resolved to make his nation a great imperial and industrial power, threw its weight behind the Boers. Bolstered by this support, the Transvaal Government bought arms from Germany and France and secured a mutual defence treaty with the Orange Free State.

In 1897, Chamberlain appointed Sir Alfred Milner as Governor of the Cape and High Commissioner in South Africa. An avowed imperialist, Milner supported the British Outlanders, proclaiming that their position was that of 'helots', serfs, to the Boers and that it was essential that they be given the vote in the Transvaal. As for Kruger, the Boer leader, he exclaimed that "it is our country that you want" With the two sides intransigent, negotiations broke down and both sides prepared for war.

With 35,000 armed men the Boers had twice as many as the British and boasted better artillery. Seeking to capitalise on their advantages precipitated war on 11 October 1899. Things went badly for the British. Mounted Boer columns soon besieged Ladysmith, Kimberley and Mafeking – where the small group of defenders were led by Colonel Baden Powell, who went on to found the scouting movement.

Boers besieging Mafeking.

Opinion in France and Germany was firmly against the British, but at home, despite the anti-war sentiments of Lloyd George and his followers, the public were staunchly behind the Government. Led by General Sir Redvers Buller, an Army Corps of three divisions was sent as reinforcement to the beleaguered British forces in South Africa.

Under Lord Methuen, 8,000 British troops were sent to relieve Kimberley, a town of much importance because of its diamond mines. On 23 November they attacked 3,000 Boers who held a fine defensive position on the steep hills at Belmont. A frontal assault was made, "apparently fascinating to our generals in the early part of the war, but fatal to our men". After a short artillery bombardment, the three ridges held by the enemy were carried "practically at the point of the bayonet with a loss of 290 killed and wounded". Seeing the game was up, the Boers fled on horseback – and for want of mounted men the British could not follow up their attack.

Private Aveling of Tipton was in the first line. Serving with the Northamptonshire Regiment, his courageous deeds were highlighted by his corporal, who wrote to the *Dudley Herald and Wednesbury Borough News* because he felt it was only just to do so. As the British went forward they were met by a hail of bullets. At the order to charge "Private Aveling who is a tall muscular young fellow , rushed forward like a madman, not to be outdone by the Scots Guards" on the right of the Northamptons.

A notice issued to Boer spies in Mafeking by Baden Powell.

British troops defending an outpost.

It seemed certain that "he would be the first to gain the summit of the targeted hill, but reaching almost the top, amidst a perfect hail of bullets and with men falling all around him, he was hurled backwards with a tremendous block of rock on him". The boulder had been pushed down by a Boer "to save his own skin from the dreaded cold steel". Many men would have been finished "but not this brave fellow, who, with a gasp, yelled to his chums to 'Go it,' and 'Let 'em all come,' at the same time emptied his rifle of its contents and had the satisfaction of seeing his enemy laid low. He remained all through as cool and devil-may-care as if out for a spree. Such example and such words from him to his chums did much towards helping them storm an almost inaccessible height."

Private Aveling was missing for two days and it was thought that he had been killed. However he had been taken to hospital where he had "a severe struggle with death". It was a terrible illness "for the poor fellow had his inside almost crushed away", yet he "was only longing for another go at them".

The pushing back of the Boers at Belmont was followed by the disastrous Black Week in December, when the British were defeated at Colenso and elsewhere with heavy losses. It was a harsh awakening for a nation that was confident in its abilities and which expected victory, but in the face of it volunteers flocked to the colours. One of them was Ralph Smith of Walsall, the father of Elsie Lee.

At the same time "a call for help was made to the Yeomanry and Volunteers". Two of those who answered that call were Troopers P. Frizelle and Thompson of Dudley of the Worcestershire Yeomanry, who were trained in Birmingham before seeing active service in South Africa. One of their chums was Trooper the Rev. E. Gell, formerly curator of Aston Parish Church. Unhappily, he was killed in battle.

Reservists from Old Hill also served with the Worcesters. Amongst them was Sergeant J. Hill. He mentioned that an ex-Old Hill man called Waldron was "the first man in the regiment to get wounded, and although he was wounded in four places, viz, in the right knee, in the left knee, and in the right wrist and left hand he stuck to his post and fired 130 rounds of ammunition. – all he had got – and then he dressed himself in full marching rig and marched four miles back to camp., where he fell down exhausted from pain and loss of blood and was taken to the hospital". By the end of the war he was well and "eager to get to the front. That is the mettle Old Hill men are made of."

In spite of such bravery, the British defeats continued in the New Year, and soldiers like Life Guardsman Johnson of Dudley realised the need for a change of tactics if the Boers were to be defeated. He defended his generals from those who "sit comfortable at home and find fault" but admitted that "it was a grave error to march men up kopjes in quarter fashion, forming as it did a huge moving bull's eye or target for the crafty Boers to shoot at; and to give men a midnight march of 14 or 15 miles and expect them to fight without rest and empty craws was a bit off".

In late January the Boers repulsed the British at Spion Kop, a hill forever recalled at football grounds when home fans talk of their own end as the Kop. But the tide of battle was about to turn. Under a new commander, Lord Roberts, the British fought back successfully, using effectively their growing strength in numbers and mounted troops. Kimberley was relieved on 15 February. Private Harry Horne of King Street, Dudley was there and he told of his experiences in a letter home.

Harry had gone to the Cape Colony to volunteer his services, joining the South African Light Horse. Quickly transferred to Robert's Horse, after just three weeks learning to drill and a few days rifle practice, Harry joined General French's relief column "and from that day till we relieved Kimberley we had it very rough". Each day they marched from river to river, so that the men could water their horses.

Eventually, 20,000 British soldiers were gathered, "one of the finest sights that I have witnessed", and as they approached Kimberley their artillery pounded the Boers. Harry's unit occupied a hill, but "the Boers soon got range" and they lost men and horses. Harry dismissed the claim that the Boers were fine marksmen, for "had they been half the shots they are reputed to be, they would have killed the whole of the B and D squadron that day, as they were within 700 yards of them and (we) were without any cover". There was no opportunity to fire back as "there was nothing to fire at. Therefore it would have been useless only drawing the enemy's fire".

The march began again, towards the Modder River. It was a hard one, for "water was very scarce. As much as £2 being paid for a bottle of water." The next morning the advance began under heavy fire. Just before reaching Kimberley "the Boers planted six shells in our line, only one of which exploded, killing one man and a horse, blowing them to pieces". On 15 February the men "began to grumble about not being moved out of range when up rode General French and said that if he heard any more talking in the lines he would keep us there till it ceased".

Then came the order to retire, after which Harry and his pals marched into Kimberley at dusk. It was an emotional scene, as "the people were so please to see us that some of them cried with joy. They caught hold of our hands and shook them heartily." The townsfolk said that they had lived on a quarter of a pound of horseflesh a day per adult.

A blindfolded Boer emissary coming to discuss surrender terms after a Boer defeat.

Iris Shakespeare, nee Hadley, of Mincing Lane, Rowley Regis has added to the stories of Black Country veterans of the Boer War. This photo was used in the Express & Star on Wednesday 1 November 1967 and it shows Iris's grandfather William (Bill) Hadley, aged 88, first on the left. Sitting in the middle is Ernest Bayliss, aged 85, and on the right is the youngster of the trio, Charles Keasey aged 84.

The report states that the three Boer War veterans were to lead the Armistice Day parade in West Bromwich on 12 November and this was the first time that they had met. Bill Hadley was a former gas and chemical worker living at Tasker Street, Greets Green. He joined the 1st Battalion the Worcestershire Regiment when he was 20 "to see service during the Boer War". Ernest Bayliss lived in Hayes Street and was eighteen when he signed on with the 1st Volunteer Battalion (South Staffs). After the war he went on to become a foreman inspector at a spring company. Charles Keasey was also eighteen when he sailed for South Africa with the 3rd battalion South Staffordshire Regiment. In later years he ran a fish and chip shop in West Bromwich and lived at Whitgreave Street, Greets Green.

Iris remembers her grandfather as "a wonderful old gentleman, and three of his six sons were soldiers in the Second World War. He always worked very hard and when he retired at 82 years, he went back out of retirement to do the post and after was to be seen pushing his trolley to West Bromwich Post Office. In his 90th year he lost his sight, but would still make sure he was in the Legion parade in a wheelchair pushed by one of his daughters, Selina. On his death his medals were donated to the British Legion."

Next morning Harry and his comrades fought all day "under very heavy fire, the whole time we (Robert's Horse) bearing the brunt of the engagement, losing a good few men and horses". Still, the Boers were forced to retreat in all quarters and the battle was won.

Ladysmith was next to be relieved on 28 February. The British strove to clear the Boers in the Orange Free State, who were organised in commandos to fight as guerrillas. They put up stiff resistance, as was made plain by a letter from John Malpass of the 1st South Staffordshire Regiment to his parents in Brierley Hill. He was one of three brothers in South Africa. The two others, Cain and Abel, were in the 1st Worcesters.

John wrote that all three were all right "but we have had very hard marching to do. We met with the enemy on the 19th and had all day fighting without either food or water. Fighting is still on but we are under cover from the enemy now. Our artillery are shelling them every day. We had a very narrow escape on the 19th for the shells were flying all around." John finished by explaining that "I shall be able to tell you more about it if God spares me to come home".

A few days later Abel reiterated that "we have been very lucky in not being knocked over. We were marching over an open plain and before we got two miles the Boers opened fire upon us, and the shot and the shell from the hills came down in front of us like Hail-stones." In the face of such fire, the British "managed to reach the kopje, and named it the 'Worcester Hill'. I should not care about the fighting if we had something better to eat. We are getting two or three biscuits and a bit of tinned meat to last all day."

In a forbidding terrain, the going was indeed tough. Private B. James of Pensnett had rejoined the 1st South Staffs as a reservist. He wrote to his brother as shells were dropping "all around about us" on the third day of fighting. He had eaten nothing for a day and had only a top coat to cover him of a night.

Lance Corporal S. Dance of the 1st Worcesters had also experienced his baptism of fire. In the attack on Key Hill, he was 'never so frightened in my life". I ran about 300 yards in all my marching order and when I got to the hill I dropped. I could not go another yard, but thank God we captured it all right." The dangers of war were made worse by "the perishing cold" and "some awful weather", so that the men "had to lie in wet blankets and on one occasion the camp was like a river. In the morning we had to go on the march soaking wet. I shall be glad when I get back, for I don't like this life."

On 13 March, Bloemfontein, the capital of the Orange Free State, was taken and then, on 16 May 1900, the siege of Mafeking was raised after 217 days of dogged British resistance, leading to fervent scenes of celebration across Britain. The *Dudley Herald* reported that once word had spread "in a remarkably short space of time the streets of the town were thronged with excitable crowds. Steam bulls, sirens and whistles at the various works were set going, the bells pealed out, impromptu processions were organised, red fires flared, and the pandemonium was altogether indescribable". On Saturday the town was decorated from end to end and the enthusiastic crowds abounded – but great as they were the gathering on the Monday evening for a torchlight procession were even bigger. Every part of Dudley was one solid block of people, eclipsing any previous celebration in the town's history.

The defeat of the Boers seemed inevitable. Johannesburg fell on 31 May and Pretoria, the capital of the Transvaal, a few days later. The war appeared to be over. It was not, as Boer guerrillas continued to fight the British. It took two years to wear them down so that a treaty could be signed in May 1902.

Tragically, plenty of Black Country chaps and Brummies never came home. Trooper H. B. Hoyte, an only son of a Stourbridge family, died in Pretoria a prisoner of war. Private S. H. T. Clarkson aged 24 was one of two volunteers of the Dudley Ambulance Corps. He fell victim to enteric fever. Private Tuson, nephew of James Wilkes of Wood Street, Tipton, was killed by a stray bullet that went through his ear. His pals carried him to the camp but he only lived three minutes. His sergeant emphasised that "his loss is deeply regretted by his comrades, as he was a favourite of them all". It is over 100 years since these men and others died for Queen and Country. May they and all the fallen rest in peace.

I could not have written this chapter if Charles Drinkwater had not been generous in giving me a volume of the Dudley Herald from 1900, which he had saved from a skip and in which were the stories of many Black Country men who fought in the Boer War. I thank Charles and his son, John, for their kindness.

Chapter 7

A DOUGHTY BREED:
DARLASTON MEN AT THE SOMME

William Pincher was like so may other English working chaps. He put a lot into life but life never gave him much back, bar for hardships a plenty. A Darlaston man and the son of Thomas and Sarah Ann Pincher, he was grafting as a labourer in a tubes warehouse from at least the age of fourteen. In those early years of the twentieth century, by the time he was a man he would have been lucky to have earned seventeen or eighteen bob a week (75-80p), for heaving and humping ten hours and more a day for five and half days a week.

Such a meagre income put him well below the poverty line which Seebohm Rowntree set in 1901 at 21s 8d a week for a man, woman and three children. And let's be clear about this. Rowntree's poverty line did not mean that you could enjoy life. Far from it. It was a level which just about allowed a bloke to earn enough to maintain 'mere physical efficiency' and nothing more. In one of the wealthiest countries in the world, hundreds of thousands of families had to get by on a paltry sum that would never give their members a quality of life; they could just about scratch enough to feed, cloth and house themselves and warm away the worst of the cold.

Beset by short time and lay offs, labourers like William could never get ahead of themselves. They were always coming from behind. Continually buffeted by the storms of irregular earnings, their wives had to make do as best they could when money dried up. They took in washing, went out charring, did homework, made and mended, and turned up meals from bacon bones, gray peas, oats, pot vegetables and the offal that the better off shrank from as not worthy to eat. Despite all their clever coping strategies too often those proud wenches had their pride forced back into their craw by having to fall into the unrelenting grasp of debt – fetching Sunday bests to the pawnshop, getting tick from the huckster's shop, and such like.

With an insufficient weekly income worsened by its precariousness, William and his wife Eliza had no choice but to rent a badly-built and unsanitary back house in number 3 Court, Wood Bank, Darlaston. It probably had no gas and was lit either by paraffin or candles, whilst the lavatories would have been midden privies shared with their neighbours.

William and fellers like him must have had their fill of the inequalities that chained them to a life of toil and moil. But that was their bed and they lay on it, making it as best they could. And you would have thought that they'd have had no time for England, an England in which the rich were so few and yet owned so much and in which the poor were so many and yet had so little.

You would have been wrong. England failed the English poor but the poor never failed England. For all its faults, they loved it still. They loved their land with a deep passion that was born out of their unbreakable bond with their street, their neighbourhood, their town, their county. That was their England. They would never let it down and when the call came they would enthusiastically do their duty to the amazement of the wealthy who could never comprehend why the English working class were so patriotic.

William Pincher was one of that doughty and dogged breed. A part-time soldier with the Territorial Force of 1/5th the South Staffordshires he belonged to a battalion that recruited in the Walsall district. Probably he was on camp with his comrades at Towyn in Wales when war was declared against Germany on 4 August 1914. Quickly called back, the battalion was mobilised and placed on a war footing along with the 1/6th Battalion South Staffs which took its men from Wolverhampton.

As a territorial William did not have to go overseas, but like the overwhelming majority of part-timers he readily volunteered to serve his country in Flanders. After

The 1/6 Battalion of the South Staffordshire Regiment in England in November 1914. So many of these men would be killed or wounded in the battles that followed; from The War History of the 6th Battalion The South Staffordshire Regiment.

strenuous training, the two battalions formed part of the 137th Infantry Brigade of the 46th North Midland Division, and as such were part of the first complete Division of Territorials to take the field.

Commanded by Colonel A. R. Crawley, the 1/5th Battalion landed at Le Havre on 3 and 5 March, 1915 and soon after they were sent to the Armentieres district where they received their first "baptism of fire." Over the next few months the Battalion was moved first to the British line facing Messines and then to the Ypres Salient, where the Allied forces had pushed a bulge into the German lines. Thence they were sent southwards where they fought in the Battle of Loos, attacking the Hohenzollern Redoubt on 13 October, 1915. According to James P. Jones, who wrote the History of the South Staffordshire Regiment in 1923, "this was their first and most trying test".

The Hohenzollern Redoubt was a powerful fortification. Located on a slight slope that pushed into No Man's Land, it gave the Germans a fearsome field of fire over the British. The redoubt itself was linked to the German lines behind it by two well-protected trenches called Little Willie and Big Willie, this last of which was partly held by the British. Only a trench block formed a barrier to the Germans.

The South Staffs were enjoined to capture Big Willie and then move on to take a defensive site called Fosse 8, a mine at the base of a slagheap. A day or so before the attack, Corporal Jack Shipley of the 1/5th South Staffords, sent a letter to his family. He stated that "I am writing with very mixed feelings. I cannot say what may happen but whatever comes I shall not budge. If I do not return from the attack think of me as doing my duty - not a slacker." That was the overarching imperative that motivated so many English soldiers – not to be seen as not doing your best and not to let down your chums.

On 13 October, the 1/5th South Staffs and 1/5th North Staffs led the assault. As soon as they lifted their bodies from their trenches "they came under a deadly cross-fire from three sides. With a rush they captured the main trench, but owing to heavy machine gun fire swift progress was impossible and the attack resolved itself into a struggle of bombing parties."

Resolutely the South Staffs battled along Big Willie and "far into the night this soldiers' battle continued, for it had become an affair of individual gallantry and endurance rather than any battle plan. Here, for three days, they fought and endured like the heroes of old, until they were relieved by the 2nd Guards Brigade."

Casualties were heavy. Of the two companies of the 1/5 South Staffs which had held a section of Big Willie, every single officer and man was hit when they advanced. In total on 13 October, 46 men were killed, five died of their wounds, 219 were wounded, and 52 were missing believed killed. That was 322 casualties at a time when most battalions had between 650-750 men.

William Pincher survived this dreadful battle in which one out of every two of his pals was killed or wounded. From Loos the Battalion went to the trenches at Neuve Chapelle, where things were quieter, and were then sent to Egypt at the end

Officers of 1/6 Battalion South Staffordshire Regiment shortly before the Battle of the Somme, during which many of them would be killed; from The War History of the 6th Battalion The South Staffordshire Regiment.

of 1915. So soon as ever they had arrived the men were fetched back to France and the valley of the Somme, where there was then little fighting.

Still, as the Battalion's War Diary, reveal, there were sad losses of lives. On the 28 February 1916 "there was a tragic accident, which killed 1 man; another died of his wounds and 12 others were wounded. No 1 Platoon was practising throwing grenades with live ammunition. A No. 5 Mills grenade exploded in the hand of the Sergeant-Instructor as soon as he took out the pin. Sgt Pritchard miraculously escaped with only a wound; the men who died were 983 Pte W. Hough and 7986 Sgt Sidney Rooker, 23."

During March and April 1916, the 1/5th fought alongside the 1/6th in the Vimy Ridge area from trenches east of Neuville Saint Vaast. Mine warfare was a major problem in this vicinity, as the South Staffs found to their cost. On 4 April the War Diary records that "the enemy exploded a mine on the south side of B4 crater. This was immediately followed by a second explosion south west of the same crater. Parties rushing into the crater could not enter; trenches were badly damaged, and several men were in a state of collapse from the fumes.

"The enemy opened heavy fire with rifle grenades and trench mortars from a sap on the right side of the crater. Also machine-gun fire from the direction of Point 5. We established a bombing post and placed a Lewis Gun on the northern lip of the crater, and dug a communication trench round to O.64. Casualties Lt. Alfred Smith killed and 2/Lt Wilkinson wounded. 5 other ranks killed, 14 wounded, 6 missing, 1 slightly wounded and remained at duty."

In May, the Battalion marched to the Somme, where death overshadowed the land and its river. On 26 June, a supposedly 'a quiet day, the Germans 'searched' the British ground with its artillery, and "between 11am and 12 noon enemy shelled 41 Trench. Casualties: Killed 263 Pte Davies E., 8878 Pte Worthington S. Wounded 9862 Pte Britton J, 9779 Pte Bird J., 857 Pte Allsopp S., 9501 Pte Middlebrook J., 512 Pte Bullock W."

Then on 1 July 1916 the 1/5 South Staffs fought on the bloody first day of the Battle of the Somme. At 7.30 a.m., after an intense artillery barrage followed by a smoke barrage, hundreds of thousands British, Empire and French troops clambered out of their trenches and walked towards the German lines. Amongst them was William Pincher.

His battalion was ordered to attack Gommecourt road and village as a diversionary tactic to draw German troops from elsewhere. This was the first attacking wave of an offensive that was over 20 miles wide and which lasted until 18 November.

Men of the 1/6 Battalion South Staffs in the trenches at Neuville Saint Vaast where they fought with the 1/5th Battalion; from The War History of the 6th Battalion The South Staffordshire Regiment.

William was in 'C' Company, which was to follow the lead companies and make good their gains. Unfortunately, the Germans were well prepared. Alerted by the eight-day long British preliminary bombardment they retaliated with their own destructive artillery barrage as the British troops moved forwards.

As before, the 1/5 Staffs went into battle with the 1/6th Battalion, some of whose officers later wrote a War History and in which they described what happened:

> The movement was carried out as it had been in practice, but the enemy's fire was intense, and from the very start casualties were heavy. The smoke screen, after settling down, drifted parallel with the front instead of towards the enemy, with the result that when halfway across No Man's Land the assaulting waves came within full view of the enemy. On reaching the wire, men looked in vain for the openings they had expected. It had been cut by our artillery, but no guns could remove it, and it remained in such masses as effectually to prevent a passage.

Fighting courageously, small parties from both battalions reached into the enemy lines but were isolated and forced back. Others were held up by the barbed wire and as Jones wrote, "from dawn till long after noon our men endured this awful fire, but the ground penetrated could not be held, and by the evening the Brigade was back in their old trenches".

Losses were horrific – over 58,000 for the British alone. The 1/6th suffered severely. There were 239 casualties "most of which occurred within the space of a few minutes". This represented a large proportion of the fighting strength actually engaged in the attack. The 1/5th South Staffs suffered as badly as any and 219 men were killed or wounded. William Pincher was amongst the dead. He was 29. His body was never found but he is remembered on the memorial to the missing at Thiepval.

William Pincher was one of eight men from Darlaston to die on that day of slaughter. Three of them were with the 1st Battalion South Staffs. They were Albert Aston, William King and John Middleton. A haulier with a wife and two children, Albert was born in Wednesbury but lived in King Street; William was born in Dudley; and John was also born elsewhere, in his case in Willenhall.

The 1st Battalion was part on major assault on Mametz. Gathered in their trenches, they lay below a British barrage the like of which they had never heard before. According to Jones, "the very earth rocked with the violence of the concussion, and the noise was so deafening that it was difficult to hear men shout even a yard away; yet, strangest of all, a lark singing overhead was heard clear and distinct, and was much commented upon by the men." After ten and a half hours fighting and with the 22nd Manchesters, the 1st Staffs finally took their target. Several thousands prisoners were captured but at a harrowing cost: 430 of the men and officers were killed or wounded. This was half of its total force.

Of the three Darlaston men who died, Private Aston is buried where he fell, in Dantzig Alley Cemetery; whilst Privates King and Middleton have no known graves and are listed on the memorial to the missing at Thiepval.

Alfred Bird was one of the other four Darlaston men to be killed on the first day of the Battle of the Somme. He is buried at Knightsbridge Cemetery at Mesnil-Martinsart, Named after a communication trench, the cemetery was begun at the outset of the Battle of the Somme and was used until July 1918. In total there are 548 First World War burials here, 141 of them unidentified.

The son of Mary and George and married to Kate, Alfred lived at 14, New Place Catherine's Cross. He joined up in Darlaston and served first with the Highland Light Infantry before he was transferred to the 1st Battalion King's Own Scottish Borderers. By the later part of 1915 and certainly from 1916, the casualties suffered by the British Army had been so horrendous that many men were not able to join their local regiment; instead they were sent to whatever regiment need them. On 1 July 1916 The King's Own Scottish Borderers were part of an attack on Beaumont Hamel. Despite the bravery of the British and the Royal Newfoundland Regiment, which had the terrible casualty rate of 91%, the target was not taken. Alfred Bird died in this action.

Men of the 1/6 Battalion South Staffs having a brew at Neuville Saint Vaast where they fought with the 1/5th Battalion; from The War History of the 6th Battalion The South Staffordshire Regiment.

Two other men from Darlaston died that first day of the bloody Battle of the Somme. They were Joseph Cattell who lived in Addenbroke Street and Harrington Leonard Eaton, whose father was headmaster of All Saints Day School in Whitton Street. Hailing from a Scottish family, Joseph served with the 'Glasgow Commercials', a battalion of the Highland Light Infantry. Soon after the attack began they captured the Leipzig Redoubt and were then ordered to advance on the Hindenberg Trench, 120 yards away. By now the Germans were prepared and the Scots were beaten back with horrific losses. Joseph was amongst them. He, too, has no known grave and is remembered on the memorial to the missing at Thiepval.

Harrington had enlisted in West Bromwich and after a time with the South Staffs was assigned to the new 10th Lincolnshires. They were given what now seems an impossible task. They were ordered to cover 2,000 yards by shortly after 8 and by 9.00a.m. to have captured four lines of German trenches. Mowed down by machine guns, burnt to death by flame throwers, blown up by artillery bombs, the Lincolnshires were devastated. There were 500 casualties. Harrington was one of them. Aged twenty, he is buried in Cepisy-Guilly, a French National Cemetery, and is commemorated on a plaque in All Saints Church, Darlaston. May he and all those who died that awful day rest in peace.

Canadian troops fixing bayonets ready to 'go over the top' on the first day of the Somme.

Each year Rob Smith, Head of History, Politics and Social Studies at Darlaston Community Science College organises a school visit to Flanders or the Somme. The impact of the First World War is studied as part of the Key Stage Three History Curriculum and Rob believes it vital that the youngsters appreciate as much as they can what really happened during battles such as the Somme - so that they may understand the scale of the sacrifice made by the soldiers.

The visit on 2006 focused on the Battle of the Somme because in July of that year it was 90 years since the battle began. I was honoured to be invited to go with the school trip. During our time in France we visited preserved trenches and craters, paid our respects at cemeteries, and laid a wreath at the grave of Alfred Bird. Rob recognises that to fully bring into focus not only the horrors of war but also the bravery of the soldiers it is essential to find a local significance for the pupils.

I congratulate Rob Smith and headteacher Andy Clarke for the thoughtful way in which they have brought back to life the men of Darlaston who died on 1 July 1916 and for the sensitive manner in which they have made these heroes real to the young people of the town today. As the last of the veterans who fought in the First World War fade away and as those who loved them and mourned them join them, then it is only through poignant and powerful projects like that at Darlaston Community Science College that the memories and sacrifices of the First World War can be passed on. We shall remember.

Chapter 8

THEY KNOW HOW TO FIGHT: MEN OF THE SOUTH STAFFS AND ROYAL WARWICKS AT THE SOMME

A heavy haze overlaid the Somme Valley early on 1 July 1916, but as the morning strengthened so the mist vanished. The clear sky beckoned the sun, which waxed in strength as the hours went on. After a week of thunderstorms, heavy rain, cloud and high winds, at last it looked set for a fine day of weather. A fine day that would become ingrained in the consciousness of the British people as the worst of days. A fine day that would witness the deaths of tens of thousands of fine men. A fine day when the youth of whole towns and districts were slaughtered. A fine day that became a bloody, tragic and shocking day from which so many families would never recover.

For a week beforehand, the mighty forces of nature had seemed to battle with the destructiveness of mankind. The clashing clouds that had rent the air had been overwhelmed by the booming of a massive British artillery barrage. It had begun on 24 June and by 7.30 a.m. on 1 July over 1.5 million shells had been fired from artillery of all types. The British high command had invested much in its policy of pounding the German front-line trenches, believing that it would kill, wound or cow the defenders into submission.

These expectations of Lieutenant General Rawlinson, General Officer Commanding the British Fourth Army that launched the offensive at the Somme, and General Sir Douglas Haig, the Commander-in-Chief of all British forces, were dashed in a devastating way. Parts of the German front-line were destroyed but the expected obliteration along a sixteen-mile front failed. The British had only 467 heavy guns that could fire the high explosives so essential to badly damaging the German defences; what is more of the 12,000 tons of shells fired a mere 900 tons were actually high explosives.

Moreover, these guns were spread out along the length of the front and were not concentrated on particular targets; whilst two thirds of the shells fired by the British artillery were shrapnel, much of which was of substandard American manufacture and did not explode. Designed to maim, shrapnel was all but useless against strong earthworks protected by barbed wire that was so thick that it kept out the light.

Standing in the trenches were a few regular divisions that had survived Mons, Ypres and other fierce battles, but the majority of the divisions were made up either of Territorial battalions of former part-time soldiers, or else of volunteers who had harked at Kitchener's call to fight for their country and who had joined up with their pals and chums in their scores upon scores of thousands. Whatever their background, the 120,000 British troops awaited the dreaded order to go over the top unaware that the Germans had mostly withdrawn into 30 foot deep dugouts for protection. They would emerge from these to mow down our troops.

Amongst those girding themselves mentally and emotionally for the forthcoming fray were the men of the 1st Battalion the South Staffordshire Regiment. Like their comrades in other regiments, they must have been heartened by the ferocity of the British barrage whilst yet feeling sorry for those huddled below it. James P. Jones, the historian of the regiment, captured its immense power.

The shell fire at the Battle of Loos had exceeded anything done in previous wars, but even that, big as it was, was merely a trifle compared to the opening of the Battle of the Somme. No such colossal expenditure of shells had ever been attempted before, much less dreamt of. The very earth rocked with the violence of the concussion, and the noise was so deafening that it was difficult to hear men shout even a yard away; yet, strangest of all, a lark singing overhead was heard clear and distinct, and was much commented upon by the men.

Going Over the Top. Many of these men would soon be killed.

Tremors from the booming guns behind them and the bombing ahead of them poured back into the British trenches and rushed up into the bodies of the soldiers. With five minutes to go before the attack, officers warned their men that Zero Hour was imminent. That was the worst time, knowing that in a few moments you could be dead or terribly injured. Some soldiers tried to block out everything, others feared the worst; some thought of loved ones and yet others looked forward to finally getting to grips with the enemy.

Four minutes tolled the officers. Three minutes. Two minutes. One minute. Thirty seconds. Ten seconds. Fear, determination, excitement all coursed through each man as the officers blew their whistles. That was it. Bayonets fixed, the Tommies scrambled up and out of their trenches into an inferno of machine-gun fire and shells.

As they began to march or run across the devastated, cratered landscape of No Man's Land, the British artillery laid down a creeping barrage – but the Germans machine gunners now came up from their concrete shelters and began a withering fire. It was backed up by a heavy artillery bombardment. The official German account stated that despite this "the strong, usually young, and well-armed British soldier followed his officers blindly, and the officers, active and personally brave, went ahead of their men in battle with great courage".

Officers and men of the 1st Battalion South Staffordshire Regiment on the march in late 1915. How many of them survived the next few months, especially the first day of the Battle of the Somme? Taken from James P. Jones, A History of the South Staffordshire Regiment (1705-1923).

In too many places the coils of barbed wire had not been blown away. Thousands of men, pierced and held fast by the barbs, were mown down by the Germans. Here and there gaps had been made, but as the British troops funnelled through them they were cut down. It was horrific.

Both the 1/6 Battalion and 1/8 Battalion of the Royal Warwicks suffered terribly. Territorials, they had been based at the drill halls in Thorp Street, Birmingham and Aston. They were moved to the Serre sector and attached to the 11th Infantry Brigade (4th Division). Here they were part of an attack in which the 93rd Brigade (31st Division) and 94th Brigade (31st Division) were ordered to take Pendant Copse and reach as far as the German-held Pendant and Flank Trenches. These Brigades included the Durham Light Infantry and Pals Battalions such as the 1st Bradford Pals, the 1st Leeds Pals, and the Accrington Pals that were later to become renowned for their bravery and mourned for their heavy losses.

The heroism and suffering of the Royal Warwicks were as great. They were deployed to the right flank of the northern battalions and moved forward with the Heidenkopf Redoubt or the Quadrilateral Redoubt as it was called by the British to their immediate right. This strongpoint was a trench packed with machine guns that pushed out from the German line down a slight slope and into No Man's Land. Four hundred yards across its front, it gave the Germans the opportunity to fire across the flanks of the advancing British. What is more, there was no cover between the Quadrilateral and the British trenches.

Written six years after the war, the History of the 1/6 was heavy with the sense of loss still felt by the survivors of that assault. The entry for 1 July is stark: "Ill-fated day. Wounds and death were the fruit of it, and to those who outlived it an accursed memory of horror. Imperishable courage inspired every fighting man, but where was the Victory?"

At 7.30 a.m. the 1/8 Battalion Royal Warwicks "leapt forward from the front line". They were followed seven minutes later by the four companies of the 1/6 Battalion but "already we were decimated by shells and venomous machine guns that nothing could silence". Valiantly the 1/8th managed to take their objective, the German front and support lines, and was bolstered by the survivors of the 1/6. The two battalions heroically went on and "reached the third line and the near edge of the grisly quadrilateral".

Private George Leonard was one of those who survived that dreadful run across fields that were like "a colander of shell-holes" and across which "the Germans were raking every inch with machine-gun fire. We hopped from shell-hole to shell-hole firing as we went. One minute there were 50 men round me. The next only a dozen. It was a miracle how any of us got through."

The Great War veteran remembered that "the Jerries came running out of their dug-outs and I had to use the bayonet. That's something I've tried to forget ever since, but it's like boxing – and I used to be handy with my 'donnies'. Once you are in the ring somebody's got to win. They hadn't worried about the holes blown in the barbed wire by our artillery. They just trained their machine-guns onto the holes – then waited for us to come through them."

Part of the Quadrilateral was also taken, but to the left of the Royal Warwicks, "the 31st Division were hung up below Serre", whilst to the right the 4th Division had been unable to reach its goal of the Munich Trench. This meant that German troops remained on each flank of the Royal Warwicks. Isolated and surrounded on three sides, they fell back on the Quadrilateral.

By 11 a.m., three and half hours after the Battle of the Somme had started, the British were in a dire position, as was made plain in the 1/6th history: "2nd Lieut. J. G. Cooper was the only officer of the Battalion left untouched, and a dwindling handful of men of the 6th and 8th was left amongst heaps of dead and dying to man the quadrilateral against counter-attacks from both flanks and the pitiless cross fire of the German machine guns. It was useless to remain, impossible to go forward."

A German report emphasised how "the stubbornly resisting opponents were pushed back step by step. Over and over they settled down again, barricaded themselves behind sandbags, installed machine guns and small mine throwers, so that they could only slowly be moved with hand grenades."

As evening fell, the Royal Warwicks withdrew. It was desperate and slow. With the Colonel and second in command of the 1/6th badly wounded and all the company commanders dead or wounded, Captain J. L. Mellor, the Adjutant, led "the poor remnants of the Battalion back". It took half an hour to return to the British lines. As those who lived to tell the tale of the 1/6 that day recounted, "four Companies of heroes by sunset were reduced to the strength of two weak platoons".

One of those who was left behind was Brigadier General C.B. Rouse, commander of the 11th Brigade. He had moved his headquarters into the German trenches taken by the Royal Warwicks. As he lay mortally wounded he praised his men: "I did not before think much of the Territorials, but, by God they can fight".

The 1/8th suffered 578 casualties, of whom 240 did not live; whilst the 1/6th had 472 casualties, of whom 160 were killed or died of wounds. Amongst them was Private John James Perkins from Camp Hill. He was just sixteen years old. Another was Private Henry Woodward from Moseley. He was only fifteen years old. His body was never found and he is commemorated on the Thiepval Memorial to the Missing of the Somme.

The losses of the 1/5th and 1/6th Battalions of the South Staffordshire Regiment were also grievous. They too were Territorials, with the 1/5th recruiting in Walsall and the 1/6th in Wolverhampton. On that doom-laden day of 1 July the two battalions were part of the 46th (North Midland) Division. With the 56th (London) Division) it was ordered to attack Gommecourt, an enemy salient that bulged out

A wounded German soldier with British troops.

from the German lines into No Man's Land, in a diversion to draw German troops away from Serre to the south. The two divisions attacked to the north and south of the heavily fortified village and aimed to link up behind it – thus cutting off the Germans. The plan failed.

After the Great War, a committee of the officers of the 1/6th wrote up the battalion's war history. At the time even the commanding officer, Lieutenant J. H. Thursfield, was unaware of the reasons for the attack: "was it merely a blind to cover more important operations proceeding elsewhere, or was it thought that the capture of this stronghold would weaken the enemy's position further south and be necessary if a general advance were to take place?"

Whatever the intention, the Battalion went ahead with its task and trained hard in the preceding months. A few days before the 29 June, originally the date for the start of the Somme offensive, the 1/6th joined with their North Staffordshire fellows to dig an advance assault trench. This was needed because although the British line mostly was 250 yards from the German front, it fell away to the left.

Engineers taped out the new line and detailed preparations were made for the new trench and communication trenches leading to it. Protected "by a large covering party comprising the greater part of the 5th South Staffords", the two other

Staffordshire battalions set to. The work was to be completed in one night." Silence was essential in the darkness, "since the slightest sound of digging would have given the position away, and, owing to the close proximity of the enemy, made the task impossible."

Fortunately the night was fine, the ground was easy, "and within half an hour every man had dug himself in, and by the time the troops had to withdraw in the morning a continuous line had been formed, from four to five feet deep, with the necessary communication trenches". The new line, however, was not completed and the next night work began again: "a sharp look-out was kept by the troops holding the sector, to see whether the enemy would take any action when he found, as he was bound to do, that this new line had been formed".

Conditions were bad. It rained heavily and the trenches were almost waist-deep in water. The best that the troops could do "was to bale the water out with their steel helmets. Rain was pouring in torrents, and from the exposed position in the front line it was difficult to keep telephonic communication with the artillery." Then at 12.20 a.m. "the enemy guns opened, and for a quarter of an hour or so a heavy fire was directed on our working parties. Those who were not prevented by the depth of

The basilica at Albert with its famed Golden Virgin ready to topple. Albert was the main centre for British troops behind the line at the Somme.

water managed to take cover in the new trench; others who were caught in the open suffered heavily." The Battalion "lost many good men, and we had received proof of the strength and accuracy of the enemy artillery".

The delay in the start of the Battle "was unfortunate for us. Our artillery preparations were such as to leave no room for doubt in the enemy mind that an attack was contemplated, and each day's delay detracted from the element of surprise." In fact the enemy replaced its troops with the 2nd Guards Reserve Division. Thus the British aim was achieved of drawing crack German soldiers away from the south.

As Zero Hour approached, the four companies of the 1/6th each had a frontage of 75 yards, and were disposed in four lines of platoons which were to follow at 80 yards distance. The 6th North Staffords were on the left and the 1/5th South Staffords behind. More than a dozen waves of various units were positioned from the line back, "and it was anticipated that they would follow one another so as to cross the advanced trench at intervals of one minute each. The assaulting troops were heavily equipped, especially the fourth wave, which was detailed to carry a supply of bombs packed in loads for two men to carry."

At 6.25 a.m. an intense British bombardment began, but "the enemy replied vigorously, both with his field guns and howitzers, and revealed the true strength of his artillery. His machine guns were also active, and directed an accurate fire on the parapets, more especially where the communication trenches led from the front line to the advanced trench." One of these machine guns was in the north-west corner of Gommecourt Village and could not be silenced and it "must have been responsible for a large number of the casualties in the advance".

However, one gap had been made and some of D Company "managed to gain a footing in the enemy's front line, but were soon outnumbered and fell". The bombers under Lieutenant Flaxman also made for the gap but the wire "prevented them from getting to grips, and they were shot down in the open". On the right flank C Company engaged the enemy "but they could make no headway and suffered heavily. For the rest, those men who passed through the barrages and escaped the machine-gun fire could make no progress past the enemy's wire." As for A and B Companies they found no gaps.

Many men died horribly. Caught on the barbed wire they were cut apart by German machine-gun fire. Casualties were severe. Out of the total of 239, most occurred within a few minutes of the beginning of the attack, and "represented a large proportion of the fighting strength actually engaged in the attack." Of the "platoon commanders few escaped. Lieut. Harley and Lieut. Dickinson were both shot down at the German wire, and Lieutenants Flaxman, Johnson and Page were killed in a similar manner. Lieut. Adams was shot through the knee, and in crawling back to our lines was sniped continuously, one bullet striking the magazine of his revolver which he wore at his side."

British troops trudging through mud and shattered trees at the Battle of the Somme.

Elsewhere in the Battle of the Somme, the 1st Battalion South Staffordshire Regiment was prominent in one of the few success of the day. It was part of the 7th Division, made up of mostly of Regular Battalions which had experienced hard fighting since the early days of the war. Their target was the village of Mametz.

Three large mines and several smaller ones were exploded in front of the German positions just before Zero Hour. According to James P. Jones, the regimental historian, when the whistles blew to attack, "on each flank from Fricourt on the left, to the country towards Montauban on the right, a long line of bayonets surged forwards. A lively machine gun fire and shrapnel greeted them" but the 1st Battalion never faltered.

Amazingly the men covered over 1,200 yards in about 30 minutes. The first platoon into Mametz was led by 2nd Lieutenant S. Potter. He led a rapid advance that swept through the village and dug himself and his men in on the farther side. Although surrounded by the enemy they maintained their position under heavy fire until noon, when the rest of the Battalion finally succeeded in joining them. Second Lieutenant S. Potter was awarded the D.S.O. "for conspicuous gallantry", as his citation read. His achievement was "of great tactical importance. Later he took part in another assault on another position which was taken owing to his personal gallantry and fine leadership."

There was a large number of Germans in the village and the rest of the Battalion "advanced as if on parade, they swept forward in regular lines, and to one who followed their track the regularity of their advance was astonishing, for the dead lay aligned as if on some parade."

Many prisoners "were found in their dug-outs, men dazed and bewildered with the awful hell of the bombardment they had endured. They said it was not war, but murder. They forgot what they had done when they held the whip-hand with their artillery in the earlier days of the war, and did not like the dose of their own medicine they had to swallow in this attack."

A trench called Dantzig Alley ran through the middle of Mametz. The defenders put up a strong resistance and German counter attacks were launched supported by heavy shelling and machine guns fire. These were held off. Dantzig Alley was captured, cellars and strongpoints were taken, and slowly the village was secured so that by the middle of the afternoon most of Mametz was in British hands.

The heat was intense, and the men's tunics were black with sweat, but "at about 1 p.m. the 1st Battalion surged forward again, and Lieut. C. de Trafford led a most gallant attack on 'Bunny Alley', a trench just in rear of Mametz, clearing it and taking about 200 prisoners". The price was high. Only eleven out of 21 officers who had gone over the top were left; whilst 300 other ranks were dead or wounded.

By the end of the first bloody day of the Battle of the Somme, British casualties totalled 57,000 men; 20,000 of them were dead. The Battle went on for another 140 days. Tens of thousands more British and Empire troops died. Over 73,000 have no known grave and are commemorated on the Thiepval Memorial. Amongst them are the names of 604 men of the South Staffordshire Regiment and 1,803 of the Royal Warwicks. May they and all the fallen rest in peace.

Chapter 9

SMETHWICK UNDAUNTED: SMETHWICK DURING THE BLITZ

It was Holy Week 1941, half way between Palm Sunday and Easter, but the religious significance failed to stop the Nazis once again pounding Birmingham and Smethwick – as they had been doing for months. On the night of 9 April 1941, 200 bombers flew across the darkened skies of the West Midlands, dropping 650 high explosive bombs and 170 sets of incendiaries. The first of them fell on Bordesley Green at 9.35 p.m. and within minutes reports were coming in of high explosive bombs landing elsewhere. Death and destruction came in their wake.

As ever the anti-aircraft personnel and the Royal Air Force did their best to stop the enemy, and succeeded in shooting down seven bombers. Six were brought down in the countryside. The seventh was a Heinkel 111 that was fetched down by a Boulton Paul Defiant. This was a plane made in Wolverhampton and had a crew of Flight Lieutenant Christopher Deansley and rear gunner Sergeant Jack Scott.

The Heinkel had taken off from its base in Dinard, Northern France aiming for an engine factory in Birmingham. Unhappily, after it was hit it went on to hurtle into two houses at 281 and 283 Hales Lane (now St Mark's Road), Smethwick, killing seven people. Forty-eight year old Amy Hanson and her daughter Doreen lost their lives at number 281, whilst next door five members of the Smart family were later found dead amidst the wreckage. Three of them were children – Freddie, Brian and Malcolm.

A member of a party of firewatchers on duty in the road told a reporter that "we heard the clatter of machine gun fire and a scream as the plane came down. We threw ourselves flat on the ground in an entry and the machine crashed into the houses immediately opposite. There was only a dull explosion, but there was a blinding flash, and the wreckage of the plane and the houses was blown in all directions. I saw a member of the Home Guard run to the blazing plane and drag out a body. The airman wore an iron cross.

Thomas Packer, a warden, described the capture of one member of the crew in Hales Lane: "I was at the post when the airman was brought in by Warden Simmons and Home Guards Chadney and Davies." He said that they had caught the German at the Oval immediately after he landed and that he had an injury to his foot and limped."

This airman was Werner Streke and he was held close to the home of Chief Air Raid Warden, Frank Atherton. Two other members of the crew Egon Grolig and Helmut Hacke were killed when the British plane had strafed the Heinkel. As for the pilot, he was Rudolf Müller and was captured in Barston Road, Quinton – where his parachute had taken him. Thanks to the sterling research of Anthony Rosser and Bernard Taylor of the Quinton Local History Society, Rudolf Müller was brought to England in 2002 where he recounted his recollections of that night. He remembered that:

> I was on my way to the target, when out of the blue I was shot at from underneath, I realised there was a fighter plain underneath me. The windscreen was smashed and my co-pilot, who was also the navigator, was killed. The instrumentation and the engine began to play up. I tried to get rid of the fighter plane by pushing down on it because it was underneath me because of this I lost height and was caught up in the barrage balloons.
>
> I feel that I managed to get out alive because the seat I was in had armour plate underneath, whereas my co-pilot's seat didn't. Also my co-pilot was lying forward trying to operate the machine gun. I tried to contact all of the others via the headphones that connected us; two of my crew were dead, Werner Streke got out with me.
>
> I told Streke to evacuate; by the time I got out it was seconds later. I was doing about 200 kilometres per hour, which would explain why I landed in Quinton and my plane some distance away. I was passing over Quinton at 0200 to 0300 hours.

Jean Higgins, nee Sessions, has strong memories of the same event. They are included in a significant new book called Recollections of Smethwick during the Second World that has been produced by the Smethwick Heritage Centre Trust. Jean "was standing in our front garden when a plane came towards me flying very low. It had smoke across its wings. I watched it pass over and then saw a plume of smoke in the direction of Hales Lane."

This attack on Smethwick was one of ten raids on the town during the Blitz on Britain. On 7 October 1944, the *Smethwick Telephone* included a major article on 'Air raids on Smethwick. Never-To-Be-Forgotten Nights of 1940-41'. It explained that "now that the veil of censorship which has prevented the publication of information on enemy raids has been partially lifted, it is possible to reveal some thing of Smethwick's experiences during the grim and momentous days of the 'blitz'. Even now it is not possible for security reasons to publish the whole story, but sufficient can be told to show that Smethwick and its citizens did not emerge unscathed from the attacks of Germany's Luftwaffe."

Smethwick lay between a Birmingham and a Black Country whose industries were vital to the war effort, whilst the town itself was a major centre of munitions production, boasting important firms such as Henry Hope's, Avery's, British Pens, the Birmid, the Birmingham Railway Carriage and Wagon, Tangye's, Northern Aluminium, GKN, Chance's and others. Tanks, gliders, castings, nuts, bolts, screws, glass ware, testing tubes and much more poured out of the factories of the town – making it a prime target for the enemy.

As it was, the Smethwick Telephone remarked that "the enemy commenced his vicious attacks on the Midlands in August 1940, whilst the Battle of Britain was at its height, and the people of Smethwick soon became conscious of the enemy's intention to carry out a war in the night sky from the fires in neighbouring towns caused by incendiary attacks. For the people of Smethwick there followed weeks of almost ceaseless alarms with long dreary nights spent in shelters, but it was not until the night of 22nd/23rd October 1940 that Smethwick received its first bombs."

On that night three explosive bombs were dropped on "a thickly-populated part of Soho. Miraculously the only casualties were four horses that were killed in a stable that took a direct hit. From that night on, Smethwick was in the front line.

General Montgomery, 'Monty', inspecting the Home Guard at the Birmingham Railway Wagon and Carriage Works.

Three nights later on the evening of 25 October, high explosives and incendiaries fell upon Spon Lane, Uplands, and Warley Woods wards of the borough. Among the victims were members of the Civil Defence Services and the Home Guard. Working strenuously, the Fire Service managed to prevent major fires breaking out "a tribute to the training which they had undergone during the long months of preparation. Smethwick now knew the meaning of the word 'blitz', yet the people remained

Cyril Caine well remembers when King George VI and Queen Elizabeth visited Chance Brothers on 19 April 1940, as "I took several photos of them arriving through the Lighthouse Gatehouse in a cavalcade of cars. I took some from the rooftop of the Britannia buildings and then a couple of shots as they left the Pressed Department with Sir Hugh Chance. The King and Queen passed within a few feet of me and the King glanced at me while I took the snaps with my Kodak Hawkeye camera, which I still have. Mr Carr, the Chemist, developed and printed the film on the understanding that I showed them to no-one. The factory was on War Work with most employees in a reserved occupation. The King and Queen's visit was hush hush. He said we could both be heavily fined if they were known, but after 60 years I don't think that matters. The snaps are not Cecil Beaton quality. To me the photos and memories of that day are of our much loved King and Queen."

Mitchell's and Butler's Home Guard.

undaunted and the mourning for relatives and friends and the sight of demolished and damaged property served to stiffen the resistance to Hitler's terrorism."

There was then a lull in the attacks, but not in the tension. For the next three weeks alerts were sounded every night. Nerves were tautened by the daily strain and by the fear of forthcoming raids. They became reality on the night of Tuesday 19 November, after which the Germans announced that they had "plastered Birmingham, the centre of the British armament and supply industries, with bombs". Smethwick was also hit badly in that terrible raid.

It began at 7.17 p.m. when the first of 350 planes dropped flares and incendiaries, lighting up their targets for the heavy bombers to drop their slivers of death. Ten minutes later Fisher and Ludlow's was struck and from Birmingham's Control Centre teleprinter messages sped almost minute by minute to the Ministry of Home Security in London. Abruptly they told of the severity of the bombing:

21.35: Raid continues to be heavy and widespread. Fire position getting worse.
22.34: New Street Station signal box, direct hit, station closed.
22.50: Chance Bros, Smethwick; Wilmot Breeden, Tyseley; hit.

In total, 86 high explosive bombs and countless incendiaries rained down on Smethwick during a raid lasting over nine and a half hours. Twenty-one people were killed and the most "distressing feature of this raid was the number of small children who lost their lives". Amongst the buildings destroyed or damaged were the Rink Market, the Waterloo Hotel, and schools on the Bearwood and Oldbury Roads. A public shelter took a direct hit but thankfully all six people inside escaped without injury. Gas, water and electricity mains were damaged, "but the repair services worked minor miracles, and the normal life of the town was able to proceed with a minimum of inconvenience".

Three nights afterwards the Sandwell district had "its bitterest experience. Extensive damage was done to house property in that area, and the whole of the fatal casualties came from incidents in that part of the borough, most of them as a result of a direct hit on two adjacent Anderson shelters by a heavy calibre bomb."

The awful experiences were not at an end. On 12 December 1940, Smethwick endured its longest raid, along with Birmingham. The sirens warned of impending danger at 6.29 p.m. and the all clear was not sounded until 7.39 the next morning. The town had been battered and there was widespread damage to schools, a church, homes and businesses but fortunately "the casualty list was surprisingly small".

Several parachute mines had also fallen locally. One landed in Warley Woods. The second came down at Avery's, destroying the firm's gun carriage department and killing three employees. Another devastated the Beehive Foundry in Brewery Street and Trinity Street Schools; whilst the fourth drifted over Crocketts Lane before coming down on the pavement close to the Council House, where it failed to explode.

Robert Slingsby was in the Home Guard formed from workers at Smethwick Drop Forgings and was made a second lieutenant at the young age of nineteen. He recalls that the Army Disposal Squad attended the UXB and "then had to load it on to their truck. The Police borrowed a mobile crane from Smethwick Drop Forgings, which was driven by Mr Rowe and used for lifting heavy die-blocks. His brave act made the local papers, there being no guarantee that the mine would not suddenly explode. However all went well and the road reopened to traffic again".

For the next few months, the Germans left Smethwick alone, but they returned on the night of 9/10 April 1941 when the Heinkel 111 was shot down, and came back again the next night. Once again the local Air Raid Precautions people and Fire Service worked doggedly and bravely, so that "the incendiaries were promptly and efficiently tackled, and what might have been a very serious situation was kept well in hand". However, there was a large-scale incident in the High Park Road area "when an enemy bomber, attacked by night fighters, jettisoned the whole of its bombs. The number of fatal casualties was higher than the town had yet experienced in one night. Eighteen persons, including some children, were killed in a basement shelter when the house above received a direct hit from a large bomb, and five others met their deaths elsewhere."

That night two Civil Defence workers were killed "whilst gallantly performing difficult rescue work, a deed which was later recognised by the posthumous award of National Commendations from H. M. the King".

There were no more raids for over a year, but then on 28 July 1942 "with alarming suddenness a raid developed which in scale of attack proved as troublesome as any which the Germans had inflicted during the nights of the 'blitz'." Hundreds of incendiary bombs and for the first time, phosphorus bombs, fell, causing the biggest fire in Smethwick during the war at a large factory in Corbett Street. Two air raid wardens were killed in the course of their duties.

Arthur Morgan's memories are also in the new publication on Smethwick. He was five years when that raid took place. He brings to mind how "we were sitting on the cellar steps and the bombing was extremely loud and Air raid Warden came and told us to leave the house and go to the shelters in Victoria Park. I was wrapped in a blanket and Mr Marsh, a man who also lived in Suffrage Street, carried me into the night. The sky was orange/red and it was like daylight. When we got into the park I saw horses from either Scribbans or Victoria Park Bakery tethered to the trees. Some of the horses were bleeding from wounds they had received to their bodies."

Female workers at Scribbans and Co beside their float for the 'Salute the Soldier' week parade in 1943.

Mary Hatton in her air raid shelter, Bearwood Road, Smethwick.

Lois Bullivant, nee Everitt, was a teenager at the time. She and her Dad were standing in Cheshire Road "chatting to a few ARP wardens when we heard the drone of enemy planes approaching. Everyone scattered in all directions, some across the road and Dad and I into the entry which divided our house and next door."

The father and daughter then heard Sheila, Lois's younger sister, "crying for us to come down the shelter with the rest of the family. What a good thing she did or we would have been killed outright as the bomb went into the backs of the houses opposite and the debris filled the entry where we had been standing. Mostly it was house bricks and rubble but amongst it was a completely made up single bed mattress, complete with bedding and pyjamas which was tightly wedged in between the entry walls of the two houses. Other debris, including great long roof beams must have been carried completely over our houses, as they were impaled like arrows in ours and various gardens nearby. Everywhere was covered in thick, grey dust. I can remember the next day how eerie and silent it was, there were no birds or animals about."

Two days later Smethwick was bombed for the last time. That raid on 30 July 1942 "made history. For the first time, the enemy used as new type of anti-personnel incendiary bomb with a powerful explosive medium in the nose, and this type of bomb was responsible for a number of casualties, two of which were fatal." In particular, the Oldbury Road and Warley Woods localities were hit. But at last the tide had turned. Britain with its allies Russia and the USA had moved onto the offensive and Smethwick along with Birmingham and the towns of the Black Country would be safe from bombing. Thanks to the Smethwick Heritage Trust the courage and hardiness of the people of Smethwick during the Second World War will not be forgotten.

The photos for this chapter are from an important new book of photographs called Dig For Victory. Smethwick's Home Front, compiled and edited by Sheila Bryant; whilst the recollections of Smethwick people are from another splendid new publication called Recollections of Smethwick during the Second World, compiled by Bob Baldwin. Both have been produced by the Smethwick Heritage Centre Trust, Victoria Lodge, High Street, Smethwick, West Midlands, B66 3NJ. Telephone: 0121 555 7278 and Web site: www.smethwick-heritage.co.uk.

Smethwick is fortunate to have one of the largest and most active local history societies in the region and a dynamic and successful Heritage Trust that has brought to life a Heritage Centre in Victoria Park. Many of the artefacts given to this centre by Smethwickians reflect the impact of the bombing upon the town. For example on display there is an incendiary bomb which landed on the roof of the West Smethwick Park Lodge, West Park Road. Fortunately the bomb failed to exploded and it was later defused by John Gammon an auxiliary policeman and the son of the park keeper.

The Heritage Centre has also been given by one of its members a German Reconnaissance map that highlights all

Bomb damage in Smethwick.

of the majors industries in the area, so that they could be targeted during the evening air raids upon Smethwick; and many different papers and photographs for bodies such as the Home Guard, and the 212th Field Company Royal Engineers located at the Drill Hall, at Broomfield, Smethwick.

So much of the material at the Smethwick Heritage Centre is invaluable because it tells us not only about the impact of the Second World War upon the town of Smethwick, but because it reveals much about the experience for so many individuals who lived through the conflict, through wartime identity cards, enlistment notices, release books, soldier's service and pay books, and different types of ration books. Importantly there is a display of replicas of the medals won by local hero Able Seaman Bill Savage, who was posthumously awarded the Victoria Cross for his bravery as he fought to protect the forces of the Combined Operations as they attempted to destroy the dry dock at St Nazaire in Normandy.

Chapter 10

A CAULDRON OF HARDSHIP: FROM THE WEST OF IRELAND TO THE WEST MIDLANDS

No-one will ever know if the Irishman William Bermegham wondered at the connection between his name and that of the city in which he and his Scottish-born wife, Mary, lived. An annealer of iron, he must have worked in blistering, grimy and perhaps dangerous conditions, toughening metal by heating it up and then allowing it to cool slowly. Where he collared and whether or not he was in regular work is not given in the 1881 Census, that vital source that allows us to grab a hasty look at the couple, but he could not have been drawing a lot because he was living in a tiny back-to-back house up a yard in Pickford Street in the midst of working-class Birmingham.

Half-way between Moor Street Station and the 'Old Crown' in Deritend, the town-side of Pickford Street was dominated by a canal wharf, where coal merchants and a timber and slate merchant gathered, and opposite to which was the skin and hide market in New Canal Street. Noxious smells from this place melded with the pungent whiffs wafting from the tin smelting company and metal rolling works just up the way in Fazeley Street. As an outsider in an industrial city, William Bermegham would have been affected strongly by the reek of the overcrowded urban landscape, the more so if he had come from the clear air of the west of Ireland - as did so many of his fellow Irish in the West Midlands.

William Bermegham was 29 and his wife was four years younger. Nothing more reaches out to us about this family, except perhaps as to the pronunciation of William's surname. It may well be that his information was written down by the census enumerator, as often it was in poorer neighbourhoods. Thus it was recorded as it was said, with the 'n' missing from Bermingham. Interestingly, West Midlanders pronounce the 'g' strongly and the 'n' weakly so that Birmingham is spoken locally almost as Birmigum – as with William's name.

This William was not the first Irish man of his name to live in the city. In 1851 a William Brimagem aged 34 resided in number three 3 house 14 court in Digbeth, right in the shadow of Saint Martin's. His surname is very close to Brummagem, the

West Midlands dialect name for Birmingham. This pronunciation emerged in the later Middle Ages when the 'ing' of Birmingham became softened to 'idg' and when the 'i' and the 'r' in Birmingham were shifted in local speech. Because spelling was not standardized, Birmingham could also be given as Bermingham or Burmingham. In the latter case this became Brumingham and then Brummagem, although Birmingham could also become Brimagem as in William's surname.

A farm labourer from Galway, William lodged with two other agricultural workers from his county, eighteen-year old Martha Burke and Philip Chapman, in the home of John and Mary Kelly. Both were also from Galway, where two of their three children had been born. Crammed into this tiny back house with them were seven more lodgers: two women and one other man from Galway; two chaps from Kerry; and one man from County Cavan.

Conditions in this house must have been stifling, with so many packed into so little space and with all of them having to share overflowing miskins, a space for rubbish, and a vile cess pit outside in the yard. Water would have been drawn from a polluted well or bought stale and brackish from water carts. Having to arise early to troop out of the city centre to whatever farm, William would have returned tired and probably dispirited late at night. Perhaps his only entertainment was to go to the Bull Ring late on a Saturday afternoon to hark at the pitchers of goods and watch the entertainers.

There can be little doubt that both William Bermegham and William Brimagem had a deep bond with the city. Were there any tales in their families that helped to explain that link, or were they unaware that in the Middle Ages, when Birmingham was a small market town, that the lords of the manor carried their name? Did they know that the land upon which Pickford Street was laid had been part of the demesne, the estate held by the de Berminghams themselves and not rented out to tenants; and that the de Berminghams had lived prosperously just opposite Digbeth in a manor house surrounded by a moat – hence Moat Row? And did they ever go into the parish church of Saint Martin's, just a short distance up the hill in the Bull Ring and look at the effigies of three members of the de Bermingham family, one of which is in the style of the late thirteenth or fourteenth century and is ascribed to a Sir William?

The name Bermingham had come to Ireland in 1169 when a younger son of Peter, the lord of the manor of Birmingham, was part of a force of Normans that had landed in Wexford to support the king of Leinster against his enemies. A fierce, warrior people who had already conquered England, much of Wales and Lowland Scotland, Sicily and southern Italy, the Normans were not content to remain as allies. Soon they wrested much of Ireland from the Irish, with the de Berminghams becoming barons of Athenry in Galway.

In later centuries and through intermarriage, the Berminghams and other Norman families became almost more Irish than the Irish. Staunch Catholics, they lost their lands in the religious wars that ravaged Ireland in the seventeenth and eighteenth centuries and many of their descendants became impoverished. It was this poverty that brought William Bermigum and William Brimagum to their ancestral home - but they were not on their own. Many thousands of Irish folk from Galway, Mayo and Roscommon in Connacht had also moved from west of the Shannon and had settled in Birmingham, Wolverhampton, Bilston, Wednesbury, Dudley, Stafford, and Newcastle under Lyme.

This great migration had begun in the mid 1820s, when deteriorating economic conditions made so many Irish people look for work in England. A growing population forced many families to farm marginal land that could not support them. Benefiting from a high demand, landlords pushed up rents at a time when bad harvests led to famine conditions that blighted the already unhappy lives of the rural poor.

Added to this cauldron of hardship were the attempts of many landlords to bring in large farms that were worked by landless labourers. Agrarian warfare erupted in the west and south of Ireland, as working people banded together in secret societies to protect the oppressed. When landlords sought to seize the goods of tenants in rent arrears, large numbers of neighbours assembled by night with carts and horses to carry off the whole produce of the farm; whilst people combined to force landlords to employ local men and to try and keep up wages.

As an Irish priest exclaimed to the French visitor Alexis de Tocqueville, if a starving man sought help from his landlord he would be met by "liveried lackeys, or dogs better nourished than he, who will roughly drive him away". But if he presented himself at the door of a cottage he would do so without fear and would be "sure to receive something to appease his present hunger". It was the poor who prevented the poor from starving to death in Ireland.

Little is known of those first Irish pioneers to the West Midlands and the

A woman and child desperately searching for potatoes in Roscommon after the land had been gleaned for the crop. Illustrated London News 1849.

route they took is uncertain. Some may have trudged towards Sligo town and caught a boat there; whilst others may have slogged across the Irish Midlands to Dublin. Here they would have taken the cattle boat to Liverpool, paying 3d (just over 1p) for a rough passage on deck. Those long and uncomfortable sailings must have been frightening when the winds blew fiercely and the waves of the Irish Sea surged powerfully.

Writing in 1892, John Denvir explained that 'the hardy Connaughtmen generally passed through Liverpool on their way to the English agricultural counties. It was a sight to remember – the vast armies of harvest men, clad in frieze coats and knee breeches, with their clean white shirts with high collars and tough blackthorns . . . marching literally in their thousands from the Clarence Dock, Liverpool and up the London Road to reap John Bull's harvest'.

From Liverpool, these spalpeens, seasonal agricultural labourers, spread out across Lancashire, Cheshire, Staffordshire and Warwickshire in search of crops to bring in, farmers needing labour, and cash to earn. Sometimes these men and women stayed on the farms but often they rented a bed in dreary, dank and low lodging houses in the poorest areas of Stafford, Wolverhampton and Birmingham.

Each day they would rise early and tramp out to their labour in the fields. At night these Connacht folk would traipse back to dark streets and dismal rooms shared with many others. No doubt they sang of their homeland and of the families that they had left behind, and no doubt many of them slept fitfully, beset as they were with melancholic hearts. But even though they must have missed the bogs and peaceful lakes of Roscommon and the mountains and waters of Mayo, and even though they must have thought longingly of their friends and kin, still some of these folk made up their minds not to return home after the bringing in the harvest in the English Midlands. Instead, they called for their families to join them in settling in a foreign land where nobody but they spoke the Irish and where they were marked out further by their Catholicism and their ways.

Winnie Spence recalled that her grandmother, who lived in Bloxwich, was born in 1857. She often talked about the numbers of Irishmen who came over for farm work every year from Easter until late October after the potato harvest. Many of the men stayed and married and the number of Catholics so increased that Winnie's father and uncles gave land in the centre of Bloxwich for a church, a school, and a cemetery.

It is likely that most of these Irishmen and women arrived in the Black Country and Birmingham via Manchester and the Potteries. Certainly research into Irish settlement in Longton and Hanley indicates the preponderance of Connacht folk in the local Irish community. Michael MacCarthy, a bricklayer's labourer, apparently came that way. He lodged in Thomas Street, later to disappear for the cutting of Corporation Street, with his wife from Stoke and their children, all of who were born in Birmingham.

Others like Patrick and Catherine Grogan passed near to Stoke, coming via Newcastle under Lyme. Living in Lower Tower Street, Birmingham in 1851 Patrick was a silk weaver whilst his son sixteen-year old William was an oil-cloth japanner. His younger sister, Eliza, was six and had been born in Newcastle. Once again emphasising the manner in which the west of Ireland people looked after their own, the family gave lodgings to Daniel Fletcher, a sixteen-year old labourer from Galway.

The corner of Thomas Street and Dale End, Birmingham about 1880.

Patrick Garvey, a bricklayer, and his wife, Mary, followed the same path. Finding a home in a yard in Cheapside, their oldest child, Patrick aged five, was born in Ireland, but they had his younger sister, two-year old Maria, in Newcastle. Their baby John was newly-born in Birmingham. By contrast Mary Angle, a hardware hawker from Bartholomew Street, must have stayed a longer while in the Staffordshire town because her husband was from there as were all their children.

A snatch of evidence about some of these early migrants is provided by the 1851 census. It records a forty-year old blacksmith called John Noon living at 24 Smallbrook Street, Birmingham with his wife, Jane, and two cousins. All were from Roscommon. Three other cousins lodged at the house: Mary Noon, aged fifteen; twenty-eight year old John; and twenty-seven year old Thomas Noon. They were born in Birmingham, suggesting that members of the Noon family had moved from Roscommon sometime in the early 1820s and were amongst those who had provided the bridgehead for others to follow them.

By this date there were significant numbers of Irish in Birmingham as there were in parts of the Black Country, and many of them no longer worked on the farms. In 1842, Mr Hodgkins, the Poor Law medical officer of Bilston, stated that locally "the occupations of the poorer classes are chiefly colliers, labourers, &c, great numbers of the latter being Irish". He pointed out that much of the town was undrained and mentioned especially that in the High Street "near to a court crowded with Irish, there is a pool of green stagnant or mud continually".

Nearby in Wolverhampton, the Irish had settled in large numbers in and around Caribee Island. Bounded by Stafford Street, Back Lane, Carbury Street and Canal Street (Broad Street), this block of decrepit properties made a distinct area that was notorious for its vile living conditions. In 1840, Dr John Gatis wrote that in one year there had been 134 cases of typhus in Wolverhampton. Of these 49 were in Caribee

Island and its adjoining courts. An open sewer ran through the centre of Caribee Island and rubbish and filth was piled up by the houses because there was refuse removal.

Gatis emphasised both the extreme poverty locally, owing to the local people "not having the necessary articles of subsistence", and the marked overcrowding of dwellings which hastened the spread of diseases. Number 8 Caribee Island highlighted this problem. It was lived in by Michael McHale, an Irishman, his wife Catherine and thirteen other people.

Driven out of their own land by poverty, the vast majority of the Irish of Wolverhampton, Bilston and Birmingham had to take on any job, no matter how hard, dirty or ill paid, and they were compelled to rent only the worst slum properties in the most squalid yards. Bad as their conditions were in the early 1840s, they deteriorated further in the later years of the decade with a mass influx of their fellows from the west because of the Famine – or the Great Hunger as it was so expressively called by the Irish.

By 1845, Ireland's population had soared to 8½ million, of which 1½ million were landless labourers. Their most important source of food was the potato, as it was for three million more smallholders. The potato was eaten three times a day, leavened with

A woman outside her dilapidated home in Caribee Island, Wolverhampton. Thanks to Wolverhampton Archives.

salt, cabbage or fish (when available) and buttermilk. In the west and much of the south there was little or no alternative to eat if the potato crop failed. At the end of 1845 and in 1846 it did so - with catastrophic results.

Food prices escalated dramatically and there was no government action to bring in wheat at a time when Irish landlords still exported meat and other produce. Suffering from malnutrition, the Irish poor fell victim not only to starvation but also to fatal diseases that preyed on them because their resistance was lowered by hunger.

The British Government acted at last but its response was woefully inadequate and in the summer of 1847 all help was ended. The famine was declared to be over, because that year's crop had not failed. Nobody in power realised that because of the disaster of the previous year little seed had been available for planting and so the potato crop was meagre.

The dreadful environment of Caribee Island.

Hunger and disease once more stalked the land, especially in the west. With so many people seeking poor relief, the poor rates rocketed. Desiring to save money and not lives, landlords evicted their poorest tenants. In 1847 itself, Alexander Somerville toured Ireland. In Roscommon his emotions were harrowed by what he saw:

> The people are going about, those who can go about, with hollow cheeks and glazed eyes, as if they risen out of their coffins to stare upon one another. A woman told me yesterday she was starving, but it was not for herself she begged for food; she prayed for Heaven to let her die and give her rest, 'But, oh!' said she, 'if you would take pity on my poor child, for its is dying, and it does not die.' May Heaven have mercy on such a mother and such a child! They were literally skin and bone, with very little life in either of them, and food. And they were but a fraction of a population wandering to and from a fertile land which they are not allowed to cultivate.

The poor were swept from the land, especially in the west. In Mayo, Lord Sligo issued thousands of notices to quit, trying in vain to justify his actions by stating that he was under 'the necessity of ejecting or being ejected'. His neighbour Lord Lucan 'cleared' 2,000 folk from the parish of Ballinrobe alone. The land robbed of its people was into pastoral 'ranches'. The evicted families put up make-shift scalpeens, cabins made from debris; or else dug scalps – holes less than a yard deep and covered with sticks and turf. Even in these miserable homes the poor were persecuted by evictions, so that here in Mayo many died by the roadside.

This thrusting out of the desperately poor from their homes was a terrible thing. Asenath Nicholson movingly told of one such eviction near Newport, Mayo.

Perhaps in no instance does the oppression of the poor . . . come before the mind so vividly, as when going over the places made desolate by the famine, to see the tumbled cabins, with the poor, hapless inmates, who had for years sat around their turf fire, and ate their potatoes together, now lingering and oft-times wailing in despair, their ragged, barefoot little ones, clinging about them, one on the back of the weeping mother, and the father looking on in silent despair, while a part of them are scarping among the rubbish to gather some little relic of mutual acquaintance . . . then, in a flock, take their solitary, pathless way to some rock or ditch, to encamp supperless for the night.

A family evicted from a cottage tumbled. Illustrated London News 1848.

One of those who must have seen such ordeals was Patrick Cion. Twenty-two years in 1851, Patrick was a bricklayer's labourer from Ballinrobe. His wife, Margaret, came from Kennelle, Roscommon and their two-year child was born in Birmingham – suggesting that the parents had arrived soon after the Famine. Like so many of their fellows, they were given lodgings by others from the west. They lived at 20, Henrietta Street with Michael Monagan, also a bricklayer's labourer and his wife, Mary, both of who were from Roscommon.

The potato blight came back with a vengeance in 1848, and once more the west and south were ravaged by hunger and pestilence. By 1851, so terrible had been the deaths from the famine and so great had been the emigration that Ireland's population had dropped to 6,600,000. If estimates of natural growth are taken into account, then something like 2,400,000 people, or a quarter of the population was missing. Scarred by their terrible experiences of starvation, illnesses, death and evictions, many Irish people fled their island.

More as refugees, the slightly better off sailed for America whilst the poorest tended to cross to England, Scotland and Wales. They headed for the places where their kinsfolk and neighbours from home had settled. They poured into the Caribee Island and Stafford Street district of Wolverhampton, the central parts of Birmingham, Bilston, Wednesbury and Dudley. Clinging to each other, their language and their faith they strove to get by.

Chapter 11

DESPERATE DAYS: THE IRISH
OF THE BLACK COUNTRY

They were hard and desperate days were the 1840s. England was ravaged by economic depression and mass unemployment. Few of the working class knew anything but the harshness of poverty. With little or no money coming in, millions suffered. Famine ravaged the land, preying upon the poor. Conditions were even more grim in the Western Highlands of Scotland, where a blight destroyed the potato crop that was so essential for subsistence. In its wake came a famine that devastated whole communities. Many Highlanders died and many more were forced to flee their ancestral lands and go to the Lowlands or else to Canada in search of work and food to fill their bellies.

In Ireland, conditions were as dreadful. The potato was as vital to the survival of the landless labourers and smallholders as it was in the Highlands, but the scale of the calamity was even greater. In the Highlands, there was a population of 300,000 but in the west and south of Ireland where the Great Hunger was at its worst there lived millions. The effects of the famine were awful to behold.

No-one knows exactly how many died of hunger and disease or how many were forced from the land by desperation and uncaring landlords, but the population of Ireland plummeted in a few years by hundreds upon hundreds of thousands. Many headed for America and as many turned up in Glasgow, Liverpool and London; whilst others traipsed inland from the ports and came to Stafford, Wednesbury, Wolverhampton, Walsall, Dudley, and Birmingham.

The great majority who came to our region were from Roscommon, Mayo and Galway and they followed in the steps of pioneers who had established themselves from the mid-1820s. Heading south from Liverpool to look for work in the industrial West Midlands, many of the Famine refugees stopped over in Stafford. It was a natural staging point in their long trudge, and for those who were worn out and unable to traipse any further it was a place to find help. As the research of John Herson has shown between April and June 1847 about 2,350 Irish people were given relief by the local Poor Law authorities.

Most of these poor folk moved on but some stayed so that by 1851 there were 496 Irish born people in the town, making up 4% of the population. A significant proportion of them came from the vicinity of Castlerea in Roscommon and it is likely that they were encouraged to settle locally by the prospect of work on the farms of mid-Staffordshire. One place associated with the Irish was Plant's Square, in the north end of Stafford, where eight of the nine houses in the court were rented by Irish families, but overall in Stafford the Irish were intermixed with the English.

From Stafford, the west of Ireland folk tended to set off for Birmingham or the Black Country, where earlier migrants from Mayo and Roscommon provided both a link in the chain of emigration and a base for their fellows seeking a life away from discrimination and death. The support given in this way is indicated in Greens Village, Birmingham, a collection of decrepit houses that had few drains and which was to be demolished later in the century for the cutting of John Bright Street.

At number 12 lived James Moran, a labourer aged 35, and his wife Margaret, a servant. Both were from Roscommon. However their children, all twelve-years old and under, were born in Birmingham. The couple gave lodgings to several people from their county. All bar one were labourers. They were Catherine Moran and Mary Brennan, both of whom were relatives; John and James Gannon; and Michael and Catherine Galvin, who was from Mayo and was not recorded as having an occupation.

According to the 1851 census, Greens Village had 189 people who were born in Ireland. They formed 51% of the population and if their English-born children were added to the total then the Irish community in the street rose to well over 60%. The places of birth of forty-one of these folk are recorded: twenty-six were from Roscommon - five of whom originated in Strokestown; eight came from Mayo; and three had roots in Galway.

Strokestown was a place whose people suffered grievously in the famine. Here as in much of the west, casual or seasonal labourers made annual agreements with landlords to occupy a portion of manured ground to grow one year's crop of potatoes. Rents were often twice as high in this conacre system as they would have been for leasehold property.

Sometimes a number of small-scale farmers would come together and form a type of collective and lease a townland that was on poorer soil. These tenants lived in clusters of houses called clachans. They put their resources together and farmed

Greens Village and the corner of John Bright Street, shortly before these houses were cleared in the 1880s, and home to many Roscommon folk who fled the Famine.

communally. These rundales, as they were known, were tightly-packed with people and usually lay next to townlands of richer soil that were used for grazing and that were almost empty of people.

With three-quarters of Roscommon's farms consisting of less than five acres, the burden of the poor law rates fell on the major landowners. One of them was Major Denis Mahon of Strokestown. Faced with massive bills because of the unprecedented call for poor relief, his agent persuaded him to pay for the emigration of more than 1,000 Strokestown tenants. Their departure would cut costs and allow their land to be given over to the tillage of oats. This needed a larger acreage than for tilling potatoes and meant that fewer families could live on the land.

Scores of those evicted and almost compelled to emigrate died on the journey to Canada, and others perished soon after they arrived. In Strokestown anger welled. Tenants went on a rent strike and secret societies thrived. In the summer of 1846, a petition of local men exclaimed to Major Mahon that:

Our families are well and truly suffering in our presence and we cannot much longer withstand their cries for food. We have no food for them, our potatoes are rotten and we have no grain . . . and Gentlemen, you know but little of the state of the suffering of the poor . . . Are we to resort to outrage? Gentlemen, we fear that then peace of the country will be much disturbed if relief be not more extensively afforded to the suffering peasantry. We are not for joining in anything illegal or contrary to the laws of God or the land unless pressed to by HUNGER.

In November that year, Major Mahon was shot dead. The murder led to a new coercion act and to the billeting of police and troops at Strokestown House. Today, the house is fittingly the site of the Famine museum, one of the most moving and evocative living museums in Ireland or Britain.

It is likely that two couples in Greens Village had lived through the trauma that beset Strokestown. One was that of William Graham, a thimble maker, and his wife Honorieth, a servant. They had a four-year old child who was born in Birmingham. The other couple was that of Patrick Gannon, a young blacksmith and his nineteen-year old wife, Margaret, a warehouse woman. Dorothy Greary was also from Strokestown. She worked as a servant and her husband, Patrick, was a metal roller from Loughrea in Galway.

These people lived in a vile environment, as did the English poor. In Myrtle Row in Greens Village there was one water pump for 53 three-roomed back-to-back houses. In 1851 the correspondent of the Morning Chronicle noted that the pump that drew water from a well was "at the extremity of the row. There had been a second pump at the other end., but it rotted away, and the property of these fifty-three dwellings being divided between three owners who could not agree amongst

Irish folk evicted from their homes having to traipse the roads looking for work and shelter. The Graphic 1882.

themselves, the pump had not been repaired." Between 300 and 400 people lived in Myrtle Row and the water they pumped up was "of a greenish colour, and smelling strongly of gas as if a gas-pipe had burst, and were emitting a stream through it". A woman told the reporter that the water was filthy stuff and there was not enough of it to wash the house. For drinking she had buy water at a ha'penny a can.

Conditions were as bad in the Black Country. In Walsall, St Mary's Catholic Church held a Sunday mass at eight in the morning that was specifically for the poor "who from want of proper clothes do not like to appear out of doors at a later period of the day". There can be little doubt that these unfortunate folk were some of those who had fled from the Famine.

The Irish were pulled to Walsall and elsewhere in the Black Country Irish by the hope of employment in the mines and elsewhere. The marked 'inroads' as they were put aroused fierce antagonism and on Tuesday 18 May 1847, the *Liverpool Mercury* reported that there had been "rioting in South Staffordshire, in consequence of influx of Irish labourers, at Walsall, Wednesbury, whole district unsettled'. The violence was sparked by a strike by labourers employed by the South Staffordshire Railway Company. Seeking to break the strike, the contractors hired Irishmen who were believed to be working for less money. On the previous Monday evening the strikers had visited the pits in the area and collected "a formidable body of miners". Armed with bludgeons torn from trees and hedgerows by the side of the road, the local men marched to Walsall.

Large numbers of Irish folk had made their homes in and around Stafford Street, especially in Blue Lane East, where Saint Patrick's Church would be built in 1855-1856. The enraged mob broke down the doors and windows of houses and some Irish men were severely beaten. The "Irish party gathered together a strong force and were about to retaliate" when the police "sallied out upon the rioters and apprehended four of the ringleaders".

Unfortunately, there was more trouble the next day. Near to Wolverhampton almost 1,000 miners and others met. Urged on by women who were conspicuous in the angry crowd they "drove every Irishman from his employment. If they hesitated for a moment they were attacked with sticks and assailed with volleys of stones." Many of the Irish were beaten and others "had difficulty in escaping with their lives". So bad was the violence that the police had to draw their cutlasses. The next day again "immense crowds" of miners and others met on the Bilston and Willenhall road. More Irishmen were attacked, but a large presence of police stopped things becoming even worse. Still the crowd was so threatening that the military were put on standby.

Further "outrages were perpetrated at Wednesbury" where "one Irishman had his eye knocked out, several had their skulls nearly fractured, many were beaten till scarcely able to stand, and it was with some difficulty some of them escaped with their lives". There were also accounts of "the contagion" spreading to Stafford and the Potteries.

Both the English and Irish poor were victims of an unfair economic system that required a large pool of unskilled labourers to compete with each other for work and hence

Bridget O'Donnell and her children of Kilrush, County Clare were amongst the tens of thousands evicted during the Great Hunger. Illustrated London News 1849.

beat down wages. The few became rich off the backs of the many, but the understanding that all of the poor were exploited and had so much in common was blinded by the necessity of survival.

Two years after the outrages, in the autumn 1849, both the English and Irish poor of Bilston were devastated by a cholera epidemic that killed 730 people in six weeks. Seventeen years before, Bilston had lost 692 citizens and in the intervening years little had been done to improve conditions in the courts of the town. The Bilston Brook was "the receptacle of all many of impurities and loathsome filth"; drainage was very bad; and there were too few privies. In Wolverhampton Street alone there were eight houses and no privy – the tenants having to use one in a neighbour's yard.

One of those who strove to help all those who suffered was Father Sherlock. The only priest at Holy Trinity Roman Catholic Church, he was an heroic figure "who carried the sick on his back to the hospital". John Denvir wrote a history of the Irish

This photo of Wednesbury pit bonk wenches is in my book Black Country Memories 2 and at a book signing at the Express and Star before last Christmas I was told by Mrs May Evans that it shows her grandmother Bridget Climes, who had to leave Ireland because of the Great Hunger and who settled in Brickiln Street, Wednesbury. Jean Mould is another grand-daughter of Bridget. She recalls that Granny Climes "was the gaffer of a team of women who unloaded coal boats at the old Patent Shaft works in Wednesbury. It was a really hard life, spending back-breaking hours everyday unloading the boats, but it was Granny Climes and people like her who made the Black Country."

in Britain in 1892 and he praised Father Sherlock as "one of the finest characters Ireland ever produced". Indeed "no man – priest or layman – in England has done nobler service for the Irish cause". His mission was helped by the fact that he had been taught colloquial Irish by his old nurse, a knowledge which helped him when ministering in the Black Country to west of Ireland migrants "who could speak nothing but Irish".

So great were the numbers of the Irish in Bilston that between 1853 and 1861 there were 1,840 baptisms at Holy Trinity. However, in the later years of that decade there was "a rapid decline in local industry and a good deal of labour unrest". These adverse conditions precipitated "a wholesale exodus of Irish workers" according to the History of Holy Trinity Church.

There was also a marked outflow of Irish from Wednesbury. Father George Montgomery, a Catholic convert, was sent there to minister to them and it was he who raised the money to build St. Mary's Church which was opened in 1852. Father Montgomery became involved in a bizarre effort to help his flock. Worried about the harsh living locally, he became convinced that a better life physically and spiritually could be found in Brazil. In the event 246 Wednesbury Irish emigrated, but sadly the venture was a failure.

Despite the losses, Wednesbury maintained a significant Irish minority. In 1872 an Irish journalist called Hugh Heinrick visited the town. Based in Birmingham he was a knowledgeable observer. He reckoned that there were above 3,000 of his country people in the town who "assert their rights, preserve their national individuality, and in every particular hold their own". Rarely did differences in nationality cause disputes in Wednesbury, whilst no longer did prejudice "shut out Irishmen from sharing in the mining labour in the district".

Heinrick noted that there was also a considerable Irish population in Smethwick, West Bromwich and Spon Lane – their presence denoted "by the churches which they have erected and the missions of which they are the chief support". In fact this was probably an exaggeration, In Smethwick, Catholics worshipped in the school in Watt Street until the Church of Saint Philip Neri was built in the late nineteenth century. As for West Bromwich, the priest of the Roman Catholic Church of Saint Michael and the Holy Angels in Saint Michael Street, actually served a big area "from Handsworth to Dudley Port and from Spon Lane almost to Perry Barr".

Writing for the Irish Nationalist publication *The Nation*, Heinrick focused on the moral and political condition of the Irish of the Black Country but he did point out that like the English, most of the Irish men worked at "the coal-pit, the iron mine, the pit-head, and the furnace". Others were employed by the railway companies and by builders "in the lowest and most laborious positions, and at a wage rate considerably below what can be obtained by those employed at the mines or in the works connected with the iron manufactures". Heinrick also asserted that there was "a considerable Irish population" in Bilston, Swan Village, Tipton, Priestfield, Oldbury and Willenhall. Outside Bilston, little is known of the Irish of these towns, and it was only in Bilston and Wednesbury that there were Catholic schools and mutual benefit societies such as the Hibernians.

In the south of the Black Country there was a sprinkling of Irish in Stourbridge and Brierley Hill but only "in Dudley are the numbers sufficiently large to exercise any considerable political or social influence". Heinrick estimated that the population in the capital of the Black Country as 1,300 and felt that they earned good wages "and, in proportion to their numbers, there are more skilled artisans in this than in the other towns of the district. There is also a fair number of men who have raised themselves out of the ranks of labour, and are pushing towards comfort and competence."

Heinrick went on to draw attention to the Irish of Walsall, where "the labouring class earn good wages" and there were two Catholic churches. and to Kidderminster. Here the Irish population was about the same as that in Dudley "but the condition of

Caribee Island, Wolverhampton, where many Irish gathered. Thanks to Wolverhampton Archives.

the people is scarcely so good". The origins of the Irish community in the town went back to the Act of Union of 1801. This brought in free trade between England and Ireland, and precipitated the decline of much of the Irish textile trade because of strong competition from English manufacturers. As a result, in 1829 and 1830 wool combers from Cork "driven from home by the destruction of the trade which was the source of their maintenance" sought work in Kidderminster's carpet factories.

There were also a few Irish in the Cradley district, although they are not mentioned by Heinrick. On 8 January 1887 a contributor to the *Weekly Freeman* wrote about the Irish in England, highlighting "the destitution prevailing in South Staffordshire". So bad was the state of the area that it was decided "to furnish the Queen with an account of the hardships the chainmakers have had to undergo through low wages and truckings."

Also known as tommy shops, truck shops were lynchpins of the iniquitous system whereby workers were paid in tokens which could be exchanged only at shops associated with their gaffers and where the food was poor and often adulterated. It was stated that if it had not been for support from Birmingham and other large towns, "many deaths from starvation would have been inevitable".

By contrast, to the situation in Cradley, Wolverhampton boasted a large Irish population and three catholic churches and schools attached to them. Heinrick declared that his compatriots in the town were zealous in religion and "comparatively well to do" – but for all that many of them were unable to escape either the dreadful environment of the Caribee Island or religious prejudice.

Chapter 12

CARIBEE ISLAND AND LITTLE ROME: THE IRISH OF WOLVERHAMPTON

Belying its exotic name, Caribee Island was no idyllic isle. Set not in warm seas but in the heart of industrial Wolverhampton, it was a dreadful place in which to live. Bounded by Stafford Street, Back Lane, Carbury Street and Canal Street (later called Broad Street), the houses and environment of Caribee Island were amongst the worst in the West Midlands – as was highlighted in 1843 in the Report to The Commissioners on the Employment of Children

Stafford Street and Walsall Street were two of the longest streets in the town but they were declaimed as two of the "most disgraceful". There was no underground drainage and "the entire length of each always runs with filth, or is stagnant in its dirt". In a one-roomed hovel in Stafford Street, a man, his wife and child slept alongside a donkey; and at the end of each of the courts of back houses there was usually a common dunghill "where everything is cast". When it rained, the dung seeped into the yard so that "the slush in front of the doors is usually of the most disgusting kind'.

Six years later the dire public health of Wolverhampton was brought to the fore by Robert Rawlinson. A noted sanitary reformer and engineer, he reported on the state of Wolverhampton, Bilston, Wednesfield and Willenhall for the General Board of Health, which had been set up in 1848 following the passing of the first Public Health Act.

Conditions were awful in much of the town. Many streets had only surface drains, whilst pig sties, midden privies and stagnant ditches abounded. Indeed, large numbers of inhabitants were "compelled to have soil tanks on their premises, and, in some cases under their very buildings, to receive the soil from water closets, etc. These, of course, have frequently to be emptied, and thereby create great nuisances to the proprietors and their neighbours. In not a few cases, and where parties neglect them, the liquid manure may be seen oozing through to the surface, stinking horribly."

As for Caribee Island, a Wolverhampton surgeon called Mr E. H. Coleman decried it as a "loathsome neighbourhood" from which typhus fever was rarely absent. Rawlinson concurred, declaring that it was a "fever nest". In Coles Croft, Stafford Street there were 41 houses containing 283 people – 94 of whom were lodgers. This was an average of more than nine to the house, compared to a local average of five. Rawlinson observed that it was a rule "that a district in a low sanitary condition is sure to become overcrowded, and the reverse is also true, namely that an overcrowded district will rapidly fall into a low, or bad sanitary condition".

Going on to Carbury Street, Rawlinson shrank from the unpaved and dirty surface and the two public privies which were "so disgustingly filthy as to be unfitted for use". The lack of sanitation was as wretched in Caribee Island itself, disdainfully described as a "congregation of ruinous cottages" with no sewers, drains, or water supply. An open gutter passed down the passage between the houses, "or rather the whole was an open gutter", and some of the houses were below the street level.

As it was throughout England, those who had so little money had to pay a disproportionate amount of their income to live in vile dwellings. Rawlinson was informed that a rent of 1s 6d (7.5p) for an old house was common and that the Irish were prepared to pay more than English tenants because they took in so many lodgers.

Certainly by 1851, Caribee Island and much of Stafford Street had become the Irish Quarter of Wolverhampton. According to the Census of that year, there were 3,491 Irish people in Wolverhampton. The men worked mostly as miners, in the foundries, or as bricklayer's labourers. Within the Midlands, only Birmingham – a bigger town – had more Irish folk. This figure made Wolverhampton one of 'the top twenty' Irish towns in Britain. But as opposed to Birmingham where the Irish made

Women in Skinner Street, Wolverhampton. Thanks to Wolverhampton Archives.

up just over 3% of the population, in Wolverhampton they were 7% of the total. This was higher than the figure for Edinburgh and close to that for the Lancashire textile towns of Bolton and Preston, where the Irish presence was much remarked upon.

It may be argued that Wolverhampton appealed to the Irish because of its reputation as 'Little Rome'. There were a significant number of Roman Catholics locally, amongst who were prominent families such as the Levesons and Giffards. The latter paid for the building of Giffard House. Completed in the 1730s, this was provided with a chapel, and next door to it the church of Saints Peter and Paul was opened in 1828. By this time Wolverhampton was also the headquarters of the Midland District of the Roman Catholic Church in England and was the residence of the Vicar Apostolic.

However, as in Birmingham, English middle-class Catholics did not welcome the poverty-stricken Irish labouring poor and it would seem that the folk from Roscommon and Mayo were pulled to Wolverhampton not by their co-religionists but by the hope of work both in an expanding town and in the surrounding rural areas. Whatever the attraction, the Irish made up a significant community within Wolverhampton, and their numbers were made larger by their English-born children.

In 1849, the local Catholic Church recognised the need to reach out to the Irish-speaking folk of Stafford Street and Caribee Island by opening a school in Little's Lane. On the floor above it was a chapel dedicated to Saints Patrick and George. This mission was later broken up, although the school remained, and with

A man and two boys in Stafford Street, Wolverhampton in the late nineteenth century. This was the heart of the town's Irish Quarter. Thanks to Wolverhampton Archives.

insufficient places of worship for the large numbers of Irish Catholics, the church of Saints Mary and John on Snow Hill was opened in 1855.

A grand structure, many of the poor Irish did not feel comfortable worshipping there. Accordingly, moves were made to finally build a proper church for the Irish of the Caribee Island neighbourhood in which they would feel at home – and they rallied to the cause, making a noticeable contribution to the building fund despite their general poverty. Designed in the Gothic style by the celebrated Pugin it was to be called Saint Patrick's.

Father O'Sullivan was the Irish-born priest who ministered to the town's Catholic and as the church neared its opening in 1866 he declared that the Irish "would soon have no excuse for remaining away from Holy Mass, however destitute they might-be of those articles of clothing which they usually considered necessary to their appearance at such a service".

The strength of Catholicism in Wolverhampton waxed with the rise in the numbers of Irish – a fact that led to tensions. As elsewhere in England, many commentators blamed the Irish poor for their bad housing and unhealthy environment, and condemned them for making their streets dangerous. Over in Birmingham one author welcomed disappearance of London Prentice Street in the late nineteenth-century as the sweeping away of a "nasty, dirty, stinking street" in which children could learn lessons of depravity; and in 1863, a reporter from the Birmingham *Gazette* damned the people of the street as a mixture of the worst class of Irish and regular thieves.

In a unique voice from the Irish poor of this period, J. Goffey responded to this slur. He was resident at 13 London Prentice Street and explained that there was no more than one house harbouring thieves. J. Goffey went on to object to the condemnation of 700 Irish condemned for the evil doings of a few. It is likely that this man was the James Gafey, a second generation Irish Brummie, who was recorded in the 1851 census. His father Patrick had been born in Ireland and was a labourer and huckster, a small shopkeeper who sold everything. The mother of James was Susannah, who had been born in Birmingham.

Other writers were as disparaging of Irish neighbourhoods. Writing in 1885, John Thackray Bunce was delighted by the cutting of the new John Bright Street and other alterations behind New Street Station for "they swept away a series of narrow streets, close courts and confined passages, shut out from fresh air, imperfectly lighted, fetid with dirt, ill-supplied with water, and so inhabited that at one time - in the flourishing days of the Inkleys and Greens Village, and the like - the police could not venture into them single-handed; while no family could dwell there without destruction to the sense of decency, or peril to health and life".

Yet it was the supposedly notorious Greens Village that was the focus of the county and kinship networks of the "sturdy Catholic emigrants" from Ireland as praised by Father Bowen. To those who lived there, it may have been dirty and smelly, but it was also a place of refuge and support. Nearby in Smallbrook Street Father Bowen set up Saint Patrick's day school in "a large and lofty upper room with unsealed floor up steep and dark wooden steps over a storehouse for vegetables with skylight and 2 small windows behind".

Getting hold of "primitive desks and a huge gallery", he was helped in his efforts by the Sisters of Mercy from Alcester Street who had since 1846 run a Sunday school in a loft in Park Street. In the charge of priests from Saint Chad's, there were also schools for the Catholic poor in a seven-roomed warehouse in London Prentice Street. Rare accounts such as this give us an opportunity to pull back the curtain of middle-class prejudice and disdain and to see the poor of Greens Village and other quarters as people in their own right doing their best to get by in the most trying of circumstances.

The Irish of Caribee Island and Stafford Street were denigrated by commentators in the same way as their fellows in London Prentice Street. In particular they were looked down upon as riotous and violent. In May 1848 a headline in the *Wolverhampton Chronicle* proclaimed: "Riot in Stafford Street, and Attack on the Police". On the Sunday morning, there had been "a great disturbance in the street". A policeman called M'Caskin "interfered to quell it", upon which a Michael Owen "made a murderous attack upon the officer, striking him several times upon various parts of the body". Fortunately, the constable was pulled to safety and Owen and six other Irishmen were arrested.

Following the arrest "that part of the town continued in great uproar". It was stated that about 2,000 people were on the street. Stones were thrown at the police and at one stage the calling in of the military had been considered. However, the crowd dispersed with the approach of a large force of police armed with cutlasses.

This was one of a number of serious 'Stafford Street Rows', but as the research of Roger Swift has shown, supposed Irish disorder and crime arose from the police targeting the Irish because of the unlawful distillation of alcohol and its sale in illegal 'wabble shops'. Swift indicated that the shops were singled out by an aggressive and paramilitary form of policing that was aimed at suppressing the local Irish and justifying to the ratepayers the need for a large police force.

There is no doubt that drink was an important element in the lives of many Irish folk – as it was amongst many of the English working class. There were 35 pubs in and about Stafford Street and they served not only as places of drinking but also as important social, cultural and economic centres. Contractors often paid out wages in pubs, and disputes between them and their workers could lead to disturbances, as happened in 1848. A railway contractor employed between 50 and 100 men on the Stour Line. One week he arranged to pay them in Bywater's beer shop, but unfortunately he had only enough money to give some of them their wages. As a result the labourers held him until he was rescued by sixteen police led by Colonel Hogg – although trouble continued for hours afterwards.

A crowd of men on the corner of Stafford Street and the Horsefair, Wolverhampton in the late 1800s. Thanks to Wolverhampton Archives.

Given the disgusting housing that the Irish lived in then it is not surprising that many made the pub almost a home. The Chief Constable of Wolverhampton himself acknowledged this in 1849, stating that "many are tempted to spend their time and money in these places from total want of comfort at their own houses; indeed, many of them have told me, after having been turned out of the public house, that the place in which they lived was in such a miserable state that they would rather remain out in the open air".

This gathering on the street, especially of so many young men, exacerbated the problems of the wabble shops. The middle class were fearful of the boisterousness of poorer people and of their gathering in large numbers in the public space. As a result pressure was brought on the police to bring 'respectability' and 'order' to the street. This led to many petty convictions for playing football, gambling, urinating in public places (not surprising given the total absence of water closets) and fighting. And if they were Irish, the culprits were more likely to be sent to prison for any misdemeanour.

The problems faced by the Irish were made worse by religious extremists who stirred up trouble. In 28 June 1858 a rabid anti-Catholic calling himself Baron de

Camin proposed to 'lecture' on the Jesuits and nuns amongst other topics at the Corn Exchange in Wolverhampton. He had already spoken in Birmingham and Walsall and provoked anger from the local Irish, and their fellows in Wolverhampton were determined to stop him. Several thousand of them surrounded the building. Some were armed with sticks, stones and bludgeons, and fighting broke out with Protestants. The lecture was cancelled.

On the next night the spurious baron was escorted to his 'lecture' by the police. When he began to speak, the Irish in the audience drowned him out. Outside an angry crowd of over 3,000 had assembled. Stones were thrown at the mayor, magistrates and police. The following evening special constables were sworn in, the local Yeomanry were called up, and 120 police from neighbouring towns were brought in. The Irish again gathered in large numbers but were unable to stop the 'lecture'.

One Irishman, Patrick Flaherty, was charged with riot and unlawful assembly. During his trial the judge, Mr Justice Hill, asserted that there had not been a riot in Wolverhampton because the Irish had not adopted an overtly menacing stance. Consequently Flaherty was convicted of unlawful assembly and was bound over to keep the peace.

Broad Street, Wolverhampton. Thanks to Wolverhampton Archives.

There was worse to come. In February 1867, William Murphy planned to speak in Wolverhampton. He was a bigot. An Irishman himself, his father had converted the family to Protestantism and to a vehement hatred of the Catholic Church. After stirring up trouble in Ireland, Murphy came to England in 1862 and began work as a travelling anti-Catholic speaker for the Protestant Electoral Union. Not only was he a bigot, but also he was a liar. Murphy asserted that Catholics had stoned his father to death in front of his family. In fact his father had died of a heart attack.

The nastiness of Murphy was heightened by concerns as to what happened to money he collected at his talks and, most of all, by the salaciousness of his speeches. Filled with sexual themes and unsubstantiated sexual allegations, the lechery of Murphy's meetings was made worse by the sale of a sordid publication called 'The Confessional Unmasked'. It was too obscene for newspapers to quote from.

Wherever he went, the vileness of Murphy's words and his antagonism to all things Catholic led to demonstrations by the local Irish and often clashes with his English supporters, so that sometimes troops had to be called out. Unfortunately, his rantings found a ready audience amongst those who feared the Catholic Church and the impact of large-scale Irish migration.

On 18th February Murphy tried to speak at the Agricultural Hall, Snow Hill. Despite a strong force of police the many Irish in the building rushed the stage when Murphy arrived on the platform. Several policemen were injured in the clashes and the meeting was postponed. The next day several thousand Irishmen threw stones at the windows of the hall until they were forced back by Volunteers.

The violence was escalating and on 20 February Hussars arrived from Birmingham to reinforce the local police, hundreds of special constables and county police from Stafford. Two days later Murphy was able to speak because the forces of law held back 4,000 Irishmen, but in the Stafford Street locality there were attacks upon Protestant homes and businesses. The next week, Murphy spoke again and then left Wolverhampton. He returned in March for a court case. As he left the building he was

Women in number 9 Court, Thomas Street, Birmingham. In 1851 two mixed Irish/English families lived in this yard, whilst a number of Irish men lodged in an overcrowded lodging house. Thanks to Birmingham Libraries Services.

attacked by a crowd of Irishmen who forced him to the ground, beat him and insulted him before he was rescued by the police.

In June 1867 Murphy 'lectured' in Birmingham. At one of his evening 'services', another misnomer, he fumed that he "would prove to the people of Birmingham that every Popish priest was a murderer, a cannibal, a liar and a pickpocket" and that "if ever there was a rag and bone carrier in the universe, it was the Pope himself". The Irish of Birmingham were enraged and attacked his meetings after which an English mob ransacked the Irish Quarter in Park Street. Rioting went on for days.

In 1872, the Irish journalist Hugh Heinrick wrote about his fellow countrymen and women in Wolverhampton. He claimed that there were 10,000-12,000 of them in the town out of a total of 68,000 citizens. This was much too high a figure for those who were Irish born, but it would have been a more reasonable estimate if their Wolverhampton-born children were included.

Certainly it seems that the Irish population of the town had not declined as noticeably as it had done in the Black Country. Twenty years later, in his *History of the Irish in Britain*, John Denvir explained that "when a slackness of trade arises, the Irish are generally the first to feel the pinch, and go elsewhere in search of employment". Thus Irishmen from Bilston or Wednesbury would travel to Wales or the north of England looking for work, whilst the younger man "by birth or descent, who can save a few pounds, prefers to make his way to America, so that many of those who have left the British iron-working districts can now be found in Cleveland and other such places in the United States".

Denvir observed another development in Walsall. Here the Irish "once very numerous are diminishing". Not only had some gone abroad but, as in Birmingham, others "who remain get lost sight of in a generation or two through intermarriages". Denvir pointed to the substantial decline in Catholic baptisms in the town to support his analysis.

The Irish-born population in Wolverhampton had not fallen as much as it had in Darlaston and Bilston, but it had still dropped significantly so that between 1851 and 1881 it had more than halved to 1,687. No longer sustained by an inflow of younger migrants, the Irish of Wolverhampton and the Black Country continued to decline in numbers.

Poor and often excluded, the men and women of Mayo, Roscommon and Galway may have been; made different by their tongue and their religion they may have been; but yet they too made their mark upon our region and played their part in making the Black Country and Birmingham one of the greatest industrial regions the world has ever seen. Neither their trials and tribulations nor their hard collar and determination should be forgotten.

Chapter 13

EVANGELICAL FERVOUR:
DARBY END WESLEYAN CHAPEL

John Wesley, the co-founder of Methodism, was a radical and challenging preacher. A minister in the Church of England who had spent time in Georgia in the American colonies as then they were, he was converted soon after he returned to England. On 24 May 1738 a sudden experience transformed him on at a small religious meeting. He later recalled that "I felt my heart strangely warmed. I felt I did trust in Christ, Christ alone for salvation, and an assurance was given me that he had taken away *my* sins, even *mine*, and saved *me* from the law of sin and death."

Just under a year later, Wesley began his famed open-air preachings just outside Bristol. At four in the afternoon on 2 April he "proclaimed in the highways the glad tidings of salvation, speaking from a little eminence in a ground adjoining to the city, to about three thousand people. The Scripture on which I spoke was this (is it possible anyone should be ignorant that it is fulfilled in every true minister of Christ?): 'The Spirit of the Lord is upon me, because he hath anointed me to preach the gospel to the poor; he hath sent me to heal the broken-hearted, to preach deliverance to the captives, and recovering of sight to the blind, to set at liberty them that are bruised, to proclaim the acceptable year of the Lord'." (See Isaiah 61:1, 2; and Luke 4:18, 19).

This was powerful and provocative language. For all that Jesus had reached out to the poor, the marginalised, the excluded and the resented, the Church had become part of the Establishment. Even within churches, the equality that Jesus had proclaimed fell before the class system, with the rich buy the right to sit in the bets and most prominent pews whilst the poor had to pack at the back, often standing. By preaching in the open to those whom the Church despised and ignored, Wesley was daring to confront hypocrisy and prejudice.

It is little surprise that many Anglican ministers, themselves the sons of the upper class, were challenged by Wesley's far-reaching message and his egalitarian approach. Increasingly, he was attacked by the Church of England, all the more so because he began to empower lay converts as lay preachers. No longer were the Holy Gospels to be the preserve of the elite.

Wesley's preaching was viewed as revolutionary and dangerous, and as he traipsed the land preaching the word of God many Anglican ministers stirred up the

Cole Street Chapel 1821-1950 Jean Beard of Sedgley contacted me after reading an article by Ron Moss regarding Cole Street Methodist Church. Her "late father-in-law, Bert Beard, devoted his life to Cole Street, in particular the Sunday School and the Youth Church. He was a Trustee of the original Church and a very active fund-raiser for the building of the present Church. In fact he performed the opening ceremony and we have the original key that was used.

"During his latter years he wrote a very comprehensive history of Cole Street Church including details of the building of the original, Church complete with the names of the Trustees and details of the land purchased at a cost of £104, the conveyance being completed on Christmas Day 1820. The building was ready for use on 1st April 1821. In 1921 although the Church had been in existence for 100 years no marriage ceremony had ever taken place in the Church. In 1918 an application for a licence for the Solemnization of Marriages was made and subsequently granted. On March 30th 1918 my father-in law Bert Beard and my mother-in-law Annie Overton were the first couple to be married in the Church.

"Following his return from the forces Bert resumed his position as leader in the Primary Department and in July 1919 became secretary to the Trustees. He was a teacher by profession and taught at the 'Iron Schools', the Brewery Street Schools and the Church Road Schools in Netherton. The history we have also contains many photographs of both the present Church and of the original building."

Jean and her husband, Ron, were kind enough to drop Bert's hand-written history into the Express and Star in Queen Street, Wolverhampton, where it was photocopied and the photos scanned.

local mob against him – as happened at Wednesbury in 1743. But Wesley was not to be beaten away from his cause, and despite the antagonism against him many in the Black Country were affected deeply by his words and began to meet to pray, worship and discuss the Bible.

On Tuesday 24 October 1749, Wesley returned to the Black Country. At noon that day:

> we came to Dudley. At one I went to the market place, and proclaimed the name of the Lord to a huge, unwieldy, noisy multitude; the greater part of them seemed in no wise to know 'wherefore they were come together.' I continued speaking about half an hour, and many grew serious and attentive, till some of Satan's servants pressed in, raging and blaspheming, and throwing whatever came to hand. I then retired to the house from which I came. The multitude poured after and covered over with dirt many that were near me; but I had only a few specks. I preached in Wednesbury at four, to a nobler people, and was greatly comforted among them; so I was likewise in the morning, Wednesday, 25. How does a praying congregation strengthen the preacher.

Wesley returned to the Black Country on Saturday 14 March 1761, when he rode from Birmingham to Wednesbury. The next day he preached both in the morning and in the afternoon, when it was supposed between eight and ten thousand harked at his message. On the Monday, Wesley set off for Shrewsbury "on a miserable beast". Late on Tuesday afternoon and a horse that was lent to him, Wesley came to Wolverhampton. He wrote in his *Journals* that "one had yet preached abroad in this furious town; but I was resolved, with God's help, to make a trial, and I ordered a table to be set in the inn-yard. Such a number of wild men I have seldom seen; but they gave me no disturbance, either while I preached, or when I afterward walked through the midst of them".

Thence the charismatic preacher made his way to Dudley where he preached to a far larger congregation. This was a more peaceful occasion than the last time he had been in the town and Wesley observed that "the scene is changed since the dirt and stones of this town were flying about me on every side". Three years later on Friday 23 March, he again "rode to Dudley, formerly a den of lions but now as quiet as Bristol. They had just finished their preaching-house, which was thoroughly filled. I saw no trifler, but many in tears."

In his pioneering history of Cole Street Methodist Chapel, Bert Beard wrote that "on the occasions of Wesley's visits to Dudley and other nearby towns, people from Darby End would be found among his congregation and they returned to recount the wonderful time they had had and to tell others of the message of salvation and how the Holy Spirit was working in the hearts of people".

The significance of the Darby End folk was made plain by Bert. He explained that the exploitation of the Black Country's Ten Yard Seam of coal and the development of an ironworks led to the growth of Netherton, as well as other places locally. Amongst those drawn to Netherton were horse-nail makers who "came from Belper in Derbyshire to work in Withymore for Walker's. The row of cottages built for them became known as Belper Row and the area of Netherton in which they settled became known as the Darby End area or the place where the Darby hands dwelt". Withymore itself had been "a green valley" with scattered cottages, where grew "the withy trees used for the making of baskets, especially pannier baskets carried on either side of the pack horses used in transport before canals . . ." As for the Belper folk, some of them had already come under the influence of Wesley in Derbyshire.

Like elsewhere, Methodism in Darby End was based upon a few families meeting and praying in each other's homes and in the open air. Bert stated that by 1810 the committed local Methodists were few. They were William Woolridge, Robert Mainwaring, David Hadley, George Hadley, Samuel Parkes, William Fields, Elizabeth Round, Samuel Dunn, Cherry Rhodes, Rhoda Darby, Richard Bough, Daniel Darby and Chafer Shaw.

This dedicated group of followers of Wesley would have been one of the many local societies that had been formed as a result of his preaching. Although he never formally broke with the Church of England, from 1784 – seven years before his death – Wesley had been ordaining Methodist ministers secretly. He also provided for an annual conference for Methodist preachers, which became a major feature of the Connexion, the central body of Methodism. The Connexion was divided into districts and these in turn were made up of circuits, to which ministers were attached. Because there were never enough ministers for the various churches, many services were led by lay preachers.

The Darby End Methodists belonged to the Dudley Circuit. This covered Dudley, Tipton, Oldbury, Stourbridge, Cradley, Gornal, Woodside, Brockmore, Netherton and Halesowen. Three ministers served this circuit, along with eighteen local preachers. But chapels were few, although the Methodists hereabouts were determined to change that situation. At a meeting of the Circuit in 1812 it was recorded that "we are now building a Chapel at Woodside. We also want one at Darby End, Cradley and Brockmore, but for want of money we cannot proceed".

The next year it is believed that meetings began to be held either in a farm building at Withymore or in a space at the factory of John Griffin. He owned Withymore Mill, where scythes were made, and was treasurer of the Darby End Building Society which had been formed to build houses on the Bumble Hole Turnpike Road from Dudley to Northfield Road.

By 1815, the Darby End Methodists had increased to 44 and five years later, on Christmas Day, they purchased a plot on "the Turnpike Road leading from Darby End

The pulpit at Cole Street Chapel.

to Bumble Hole, and in front of the road leading from Dudley to Withymore . . ." The land was sold for £104 by Elizabeth Griffin, the widow of James of Withymore Mill, and fourteen trustees were enjoined that the proposed Methodist chapel should be for a preacher who "shall preach no other doctrine than those which are contained in certain Notes upon the New Testament and the first four volumes of Sermons published by John Wesley".

The trustees seem to have been mostly small gaffers and skilled workers. Five of them were coal masters, one of whom was from Tipton – although it needs to be borne in mind that many mines were small-scale concerns in this period in the Black Country. Of the rest two were maltsters, one was a flour dealer in Dudley, one was a fendermaker, one was a scythesmith of Rowley, one was an ironmaster, and two were cordwainers – shoemakers and makers of leather objects. The term cordwainer arose from the practice of using Spanish leather from Cordoba.

Work on the new chapel was supported strongly by Francis Downing, an ironmaster and justice of the peace who was mayor of Dudley in 181, 1819 and 1831, and by Madame Treffry. She was a wealthy woman who was one of the founder members of Methodism locally. Building went on apace and the much-needed place of worship was opened as Darby End Wesleyan Chapel on 1 April 1821. It was a squareish building almost as wide as it was long, measuring as it did 40 foot by 36 foot. Great beams spanned the building and it boasted a gallery held up by iron pillars. Two hundred and fifty worshippers could be accommodated and as Bert stresses, their attention was held by preachers who moved freely along the wide, box-like pulpit.

In this way, "no part of the congregation should be neglected, neither was a member allowed to sleep for they banged on the pulpit to emphasise the points of their sermons, and the voice was such that the people could stand outside and follow the sermons distinctly. The congregations were also kept awake by the members themselves who interspersed the sermon with loud shouts of 'Praise the Lord', 'Hallelujah', 'That's right brother', 'Jesus saves', etc."

The Evangelical fervour of these early Methodists is reminiscent of the enthusiasm and fervour at Black led churches today, but for all the vigour and gusto of the sermons there was a sense of humour. Bert relates how a lean-to vestry was soon added, from which "one door led into the Chapel and another led directly to the pulpit. One worthy speaking of this arrangement said it was an exciting introduction to the service to watch the preacher growing out of the pulpit, and, if he happened to be bald, it was like the raising of the full moon on a pleasant Sunday evening".

Amongst the earliest of the active Methodists were members of the Walker, Higgs and Wycherley families. The latter continued to play a leading role throughout the nineteenth century. In 1847, the fifteen-year old Aylmer Wycherley received his first-class ticket as a member of the Chapel, along with his friend Francis Clayton Downing.

Brother Wycherley, as Bert calls him, became a superintendent of the Sunday School, for which he had a "special fitness". He possessed "those rare gifts and graces necessary – very genial in his disposition, courteous, ever ready to give an encouraging word to his teachers".

For 27 years Aylmer was a leader of a Chapel society that met on Thursday evenings and he was "always pleased to hear of conquests and victories achieved by his members. Oh! The joy that filled his soul on 16th January 1879 when a Mrs Guest, in giving her experience, remarked that on the previous Thursday, returning from class, she found four persons in the house playing cards. She told them that she would burn them, and burn them she did. Her son threatened to burn her Bible. The poor woman went to God with her case, and when on Saturday evening she was preparing for the Sabbath, her son, instead

Aylmer Wycherley, a stalwart of the Cole Street Chapel from the mid-1800s.

of burning her Bible presented her with a new Hymn Book. 'That's it, sister', said her leader, 'look ever to God and He will carry you through. Go on until glory shall crown what grace has begun in your soul'."

Aylmer's brother, John, was another key figure. It was said of him that "he was one of the grandest Class Leaders that ever adorned a Methodist Chapel. An honoured and revered Spiritual Father and friend." Thanks to Bert's instinctive approach to writing the history of the Cole Street Chapel we can hear the words of these early Methodists, most of whom were working people, and whose voices are so hushed in traditional histories. Their use of brother and sister to him or her no matter how high nor so humble calls out to us of their democratic ways and helps us to understand how trade unions organisation so often emerged from Methodist Chapels.

Descendants of Aylmer Wycherley.

The Sunday School of which Aylmer was superintendent met for a number of years in the Chapel itself. Then in 1859 the trustees were given a site next door following the marriage of Helena Griffin-Walker and Thomas Frederick Higgs, a surgeon. Both were Chapel members and it seems that Helena was a descendant of the Griffins who had sold the land for the chapel. Often the children of the district would watch the builders at work on their Sunday School and "one of the bricklayers one day invited a number of them to lay a brick, with the hope, he said, 'as they had helped to build the school, so, when they attended they would build their lives in the love of Jesus Christ'." The Sunday School opened in August 1861 and it proved to be a focal point for the children of Darby End.

Chapter 14

CENTRE OF LIFE:
COLE STREET CHAPEL

Emerging from a devoted band of followers of John Wesley, the Darby End Wesleyan Chapel became one of the most important institutions locally. With their own place of worship from 1821, the congregation grew strongly and 40 years later a Sunday School was opened next to the chapel. A two-storey building with thick walls, it had a 39 foot long and 21 foot wide room on each floor. The upstairs was for girls and the ground floor was for boys. In his deeply informed and knowledgeable history of the Cole Street Chapel as it was also known, Bert Beard explained that:

> There were two fire-places in each room, but these provided insufficient to heat so large a room and were soon replaced by large iron stoves, one in each department. These were well stoked and would sometimes get red hot. Although children would crowd round them before school commenced, sometimes burning sweets on the hot iron to give them an extra strong taste, no accident resulted from their use although there was protecting guard around them.

Herein lies the joy in reading Bert's account of the chapel – the way in which he brings in day-to-day occurrences like the burning of sweets that bring to life the worshippers of the past and make them real to us across the gap of time. There was a small cupola in the roof of the Sunday School in which hung a bell that was rung "vigorously for about ten minutes before the time of each service and also on all special occasions connected with the Chapel. It was misused on one occasion when some political enthusiasts wished to celebrate a Liberal victory at the Parliamentary election of 1906."

After 1870, school boards were set up across the country. Each covered a specific area and was enjoined to build day schools and so provide education in localities where there were no day schools affiliated to the Church of England or Non-Conformists. As their name suggests, day schools brought in children daily – Monday to Friday. In Netherton, the school board decided to make use of the Sunday School premises of the Darby End Chapel.

The headmaster was James Golding and one of the pupil teachers was Fred Green, a scholar at the Sunday School, who afterwards entered the Methodist Ministry. The dual purpose of the building did lead to problems. The Sunday School caretaker was "not a very strong man physically – but one who, like other caretakers we have had, did much for the love of the work rather than for the pay he received".

The Day School also had a caretaker, "a strong, hefty type of person. The two did not work well together with the constant changing of furniture each weekend. While one sweated and struggled the other would walks up and down the stairs with comparative ease, and, the pay of one was more than the pay of the other." Later the Day Schools moved to Cinder Bank Netherton.

Bert Beard, sitting, with William Collins. In 1911 Bert became Superintendent of the new Primary Department of the Sunday School and William became secretary.

Notwithstanding such difficulties, the enthusiastic work of the members made the "Chapel the centre of life in the district". As Bert observed, there were few attractions compared with today. There was an occasional cock fight at the foot of the Rowley Hills and it was said that "on Sundays men could be seen with a Hymn Book and a Bible under their arms making their way to the religious service, while others could be seen with a cock under each arm on their way to the cockpit".

Sometimes there might be the visit of street juggler might visit, a man with a dancing bear or a strong man with a cart wheel on his head, "but it was the meetings at the Chapel or Sunday School, with the occasional concert, that attracted the people". Mind you not everyone was drawn to worship. Bert recounted the tale of a Cottage Prayer Meeting at the home of a woman in Double Row. A neighbour went to the pub where the husband was drinking and told him what was happening. Angered the bloke exclaimed "We'll soon clear that lot!" He marched grimly homeward and "seizing a chopper from the back yard, he pushed his way into the house, brandishing the chopper. Needless to say, the members were soon on their way back to the Chapel to continue uninterrupted prayers."

Over time facilities in the Chapel were improved, with wider seating, gas lighting instead of candles, and two lean-to vestries. The members were noted for their ability to sing the most awkward metres of any hymn, whilst Harvest Festivals "were quite an event" with a grand supply of fruit and bread and "the front of the whole gallery lined with hanging leeks, celery, bunches of carrots and parsnips and onions. The Harvest tea was a homely gathering and as many as a hundred would sit down to rejoice in God's gift to mankind".

By 1891 almost 400 children attended Sunday School. A great band of dedicated teachers were supervised by John and Abner Wycherley in the girls' school and by John Greaves and Joseph Wycherley in the boys' school. The general secretary was William Henry Beard. Because of the large numbers, the senior classes were transferred to the Chapel and became the Adult Bible Class. Some of the young men also started a cricket team and a football side, whilst in 1896 a Death Club was formed. It continued until 1936.

This was a vital thing. Working-class people lived in dread of a pauper's burial. Though having little in life they rightly feared a death that would make them unknown hereafter. The membership fee was sixpence and £2 was paid to the next of kin of the deceased. In an important show of respect, twelve chosen members attended the funeral, each of whom wore a purple sash, and afterwards a tea was provided at the Chapel.

Five local preachers. William H. Beard is standing in the centre.

Youth Church members holding a service on the Clent Hills. Bert wrote that the Youth Church was "one of the bright spots in the life of the church since the war".

Amongst the other organisations attached to the Chapel was a Band of Hope for children. Formed in 1898, this sought to sign up folk to the cause of temperance and it owed much to the keenness of William Beard, Joseph Nock, Lucy Griffiths and Harry Wycherley. Each Friday night the children were urged to abstain from alcohol and take a pledge to do so and they were encouraged to perform music, solos and recitations. Dryly, Bert noted that "one evening the offers were so many and there was such a rush to have names down, that the secretary, whose job it was to make out the evening's programme, had no time to check the suitability of items for the meeting and one soloist sang 'Little brown jug, don't I love you'. It took a little tack on the part of the leader, Brother Beard, to draw a lesson on temperance from the song."

By this time, mining operations locally were causing problems to the Chapel buildings. The Half Mile Gutter Pit near to the Halesowen Road and opposite Church Street had moved in the direction of the Chapel, as had George Dunn's Pit on the south side of Bishton Bridge, Halesowen Road. In fact one road from this pit travelled towards Withymoor Fields and later destroyed Magpie Row. Because of subsidence caused by the pits, the Trustees of the Chapel had to take action, binding the buildings with iron rods.

As the twentieth century beckoned, thoughts turned to increasing then accommodation of the Chapel by 350 and fundraising began. One event featured a donkey that was fetched up to the top schoolroom. At a price people could ride the animal and "entering into the spirit of the evening one daring individual decided to ride with his face to the donkey's tail, but when he caught hold of the donkey's tail, the animal gave a sudden and unexpected kick, and, to the amusement of all present, the rider found himself unseated".

On another occasion, two members who were neighbours in Church Road bought a goat with the intention of holding a goat supper. They took the beast home and tied it up in the brewhouse they shared. The next morning at six o'clock they checked the goat was alright before they went to work, but "unfortunately, when their wives went to use the brewhouse, the goat was in a very unfriendly mood, and whenever they ventured too near the goat turned to butt them out. They were terrified. One can imagine the greetings the two husbands received when they returned, 'Get that thing out of there', they demanded. The goat supper was duly held and enjoyed by all."

Work on the changes to the Chapel began in 1903 and in September of that year a new trust was formed, given that some of the existing trustees had died. The first group of trustees in the 1820s had been mostly small gaffers and skilled men. By contrast, the later trustees were more firmly working class in their make up. There was one labourer, four chain testers, a miner, a banksman and a white glaze setter. Of the others there was a clerk, a grocer, two agents and an ironmaster. He was Edward Clayton Downing – whose family had been associated with the Chapel from its beginnings.

Two years previously, the Netherton Sunday School Union had agreed that there should only be one Anniversary Service locally on the second Sunday in July. Previously the Sunday School at Darby End Wesleyan Chapel had held its service in August. Bert remembered that "it was the practice of the school to make a processional tour of the district. The hymns we sang are still popular today. Our procession was headed by a banner bearing the name of the school and the inscription 'Feed My Lambs'. The school would meet at 8.30 and proceed through Bumble Hole (now St Peter's Road) into Northfield Road, to St John Street, Hill Street, Hampton Street, Church Road, Cradley Road, North Street, Halesowen Road and along Cole Street back to school in time for the morning service at 10.30."

Bert stressed that in the early years of the twentieth century, the members of the Chapel met so frequently "that they really valued one another's friendship; they referred to one another as brother and sister. They were devoted to the Chapel and it had to be something very exceptional to induce them to attend another Chapel when there was a service at their own. The officers took their duties seriously, allowing nothing to interfere with the faithful execution of their duties as part of their work in the service of the Master they served." The week was full: Monday was Prayer Meeting and the Wesley Guild; Tuesday was a Bible Study Class; Wednesday was a Preaching Service and Choir Practice; Thursday was Class Meetings; Friday was the Band of Hope; and Saturday was an Improvement Class.

An ordinary Sunday involved School; the morning service, after which there was tract distribution; and afternoon School "and very often an experience meeting after School when Joseph Massey and other friends from Old Hill Wesley would come panting in to tell of what the Lord had done for them. Following this at 5.15 there was either an open air meeting or a prayer meeting and then a service at 6 o'clock. The stewards "would allow nothing to interfere with the Lord's Day, closing with a meeting for prayer. The prayers were always said upon the knees. The prayers, interspersed with spontaneous singing, seldom ended before 9 o'clock."

Bert's powerful evocation of Methodist life was infused with his own experiences. He stated that our forefathers had one thing in their religious life ampler than we today – "the blessed element of silence. What peace pervaded the old Sabbath – what reverent stillness in the House of God". In his own home he remembered that "immediately after dinner, before the table was cleared, we would have a few verses from the Scriptures and then would kneel at our chairs while father and sometimes mother would offer prayer's for God's blessing upon the home, putting our lives in His care. Always the prayer had a special part for the Chapel and the Sunday School at Darby End."

Bert himself was appointed a teacher at the Sunday School in 1908. He was barely fifteen and had been helping for two years previously. Soon after, Bert was invited to allow his name to go forward to the Local Preachers' Meeting. This was the first step in him becoming a preacher. He declined the offer, preferring to devote his time to Sunday School. Bert made a study of Sunday School and gave lectures on this subject at Darby End and other places on the Circuit. He also became secretary of the Wesley Guild.

Another leading figure was Joseph Bloomer of Quarry Bank. He was appointed organist in 1910, the organ itself having only been installed a few years before. Under Joseph's leadership "the choir attained a high standard of efficiency and contributed practically every Sunday evening to the worship with an anthem. The rendering of the 'Messiah' and other great musical works became events in the life of the Chapel. Two soloists who were frequently invited on these occasions were Madame Aston (Dudley) and Jessie Hackett (Halesowen)."

Youth Church Members outside the Cole Street Youth Church.

Although the Chapel had existed for almost 100 years, no marriage had taken place there. Members had tended to marry at Saint Edmund's Church, Dudley. But in 1918 the Chapel was licensed for marriages and the first couple to wed there was that of Bert Beard and Annie Overton. The date was 30 March 1918. Annie's family were also active Chapel members. Abner Overton was general secretary of the Sunday Schools and was a man of "exceptional quality".

Bert, who had served in the First World War, continued to work for the good of the Chapel, becoming first secretary and then treasurer to the trustees and to the Sunday School, and in 1925 he became a trustee himself. A year later he was appointed superintendent of the Sunday School. He went on to become secretary of the Netherton Sunday School Union.

With the union of the Wesleyan Methodists, United Methodists and Primitive Methodists in 1932, the name Wesleyan was dropped from the Chapel and it became the Cole Street Methodist Chapel. Seven years later, because of the war with Germany, the Sunday School building was taken over by the authorities as a Rest Centre.

After the war and along with other churches, the Chapel found itself striving to counter the "ever-growing attractions to Christian work. The growing popularity of the cinema and theatre, the attractions of sport and motor-coach tours, the greater search for education in night schools" all made more difficult attendance at Chapel in the week. Despite this, lay preachers remained a lively element in Black Country Methodism. One was a cobbler "who could be seen in his shop with the Bible or

The new Cole Street Church.

some religious book to read as he worked. Whenever he preached at the Chapel one could be sure of being taken from Genesis to Revelation. He may not have been able to preach a theological sermon, but he knew his Bible and needed no notes and never had to pause for the words he quoted."

Another preacher could never stand still in the pulpit, "but moved from side to side gesticulating with his arms as he tended to drive home some point. On one occasion his actions were so vigorous that his cuff landed amongst the congregation, much to their amusement." Then there was the preacher who always preached to the empty seats on then left of the pulpit, and another who was noted for "always having his finger and thumb in his waistcoat pocket". The reason why was discovered when he came to the Chapel the Sunday after one of his sermons "to see if anyone had found a sovereign which he had lost from his waistcoat pocket".

For all the difficulties posed by post-war society, Bert Beard remained a faithful member of the Chapel. With one short gap, he stayed on as general superintendent of the Sunday School until 1956, and a year later he handed over his role as treasurer. By this time, the old Chapel had been demolished as it had become a danger to the public because of mining subsidence. The last service was held on 14 May 1950. The Chapel was garlanded with flowers and "many tears were shed as nearly 130 years of grand history came to an end". The members rose to the challenge and built a new chapel.

The President of the Methodist Conference, W. E. Sangster, wrote to the members of his sorrow, but comforted himself with this: "no pick or shovel can really undermine the Church of God. The real Church is in the hearts of people." Such words could have been written for Bert Beard himself. Cole Street Chapel was in his heart and nothing could undermine his devotion to reaching out to young people with the Word of God. And Bert still reaches out, for through his inspired history of Cole Street Chapel he will let generations yet unborn know the lives and deeds of the Methodists of Darby End. He did his job well.

Chapter 15

BUILT BY FAITH:
LEA ROAD CHURCH

John Reynolds of Saint Peter's Collegiate Church, Wolverhampton was a man and minister who did not bridle his tongue for fear of controversy. Independent of thought, strong of mind and firm of opinion, he was regarded as a Puritan, someone who dissented from the doctrines of the Church of England because they were felt to be too close to Roman Catholicism. Instead, Reynolds harked to those who asserted the final authority of scripture, salvation by faith alone and predestination – that is, the belief that an elect group were predestined by God to be saved with divine aid.

The English Civil War appeared to vindicate the Puritans, for they had played a crucial role in the Parliamentarian victory that had swept from power the king. Puritanical ministers were now favoured in the Anglican Church, but with Restoration of Charles II in 1660, there was a reaction against them. John Reynolds

Stone laying at Lea Road Church in 1904.

was one of those ejected from his living. In 1662 he was replaced by someone more supportive of the tenets of the Church of England, and in the Parish Registers of Saint Peter's he wrote succinctly, "here endeth the exercise of Mr Reynolds".

Pushed out from the church, Reynolds attachment to Puritan values and Dissent was not stemmed, nor did he hush his words in support of his faith. He remained locally as a doctor and became embroiled in a fierce argument with Richard Bracegirdle, another doctor who was a pillar of the Anglican Church. During their debate, Reynolds declared that Non-Conformists like himself "were not so contemptible for Number and Quality" and he praised Oliver Cromwell. It was an unwise thing to do, given that Cromwell had led the Parliamentarian forces to victory and was seen as responsible for the beheading of the king's father, Charles I. Bracegirdle wrote tittle-tattling to the Dean of Wolverhampton. Indignant the Dean hurried to the King "as if it were the discovery of a Treason".

Undaunted, Reynolds stuck fast to his beliefs and tradition names him as the founder of Non-Conformity in Wolverhampton. He died in 1683, six years before the Act of Toleration gave some respite to Dissenters, and from 1701 those who agreed with him gathered to worship at the Old Meeting House in John Street. In its Register Book Reynolds is given as the congregation's first pastor and later he was praised as "the father of this congregation of Dissenters".

The Dissenters of Wolverhampton were small in number, but as elsewhere in the country, the eighteenth century saw them rent by religious controversy. Under the minister, Joseph Pearson, the John Street Chapel became associated with Unitarians. Upholding the oneness of God and the essential unity of humankind and of creation, they angered those worshippers who believed in the Trinity of God the Father, God the Son or God the Holy Ghost broke away.

It was an acrimonious affair. The Manders, who were even then making their mark on the life of Wolverhampton, were prominent amongst the Trinitarians. Gerald Mander wrote a fine and most important history of Wolverhampton in 1960, and in another of his works he described how "at the John Street chapel itself, violent scenes took place during which it was successively occupied and reoccupied by the warring parties under respectively the Manders and the Pearsons. The Rev. William Jameson found the doors locked against him on 24 April 1781; the rioters assembled in the chapel in 1791, and hooted; and then the Socinian Unitarians shouted abuse on Sunday 6 October 1816, and followed their precedent of barring out the minister on the 19 October, when the Trinitarian Calvinists forced an entry the next day, and tumult reigned."

Eventually, the Trinitarians broke away. The majority, including the Manders, set up their own church in Grey Pea Walk (later Temple Street) in 1782. However, a minority made their base in a former barn in Pountney's Fold, off Dudley Street, until they built a new chapel in Princess Street in 1800.

John Mander, a successful manufacturer and staunch Non-Conformist, began to transfer his allegiance. The Princess Street minute-book noted "Mr. and Mrs. Benjamin Mander and Mr. John Mander sit down with us as occasional members, considering themselves members of the church at [Grey Pea Walk]"; but by 1819 the three of them were admitted as full and regular members at Princess Street.

Within a few years this structure itself had become too small for the congregation and it was sold to John Mander for £400, which sum went towards a building fund. The premises then became the public offices of Wolverhampton, where the town commissioners and the justices of the peace later carried on their affairs. Afterwards the old chapel was used by a carrying company and then was converted into the printing offices of the *Chronicle* and *Express* newspapers.

John Mander took a pivotal role in securing the land for the replacement chapel in Queen Street, close to Market Street, in 1812. It was opened a year later as a Congregational Church. In his history of the Queen Street Congregationalists, Henry Arthur May explained that "In order to lighten the burden of finance, Mr. John Mander retained the basement of the new building. Subsequently this came into unsympathetic hands, and to the scandal of the church, was let for storing wine and spirits. At the side of the chapel in Market Street, there was a large rolling way for the purpose of taking casks and barrels in and out of the cellar. One morning it was found that a wag had written on the cellar doors the following lines:

There are spirits above and spirits below;
There are spirits of joy and spirits of woe.
The spirits above are spirits divine;
The spirits below are spirits of wine."

Often seen more of a movement than as a denomination, Congregationalists trace their origins to the Independents or Separatists of the seventeenth century. Essentially they believed that a particular congregation was completely self-governing under God, choosing its own minister and disciplining itself. This independence meant that the congregation neither needed nor acknowledged a hierarchy of authority, such as bishops in the Church of England or the regional and national synod of elders as in Presbyterianism.

Early Congregationalists were foremost amongst the emigrants on the Mayflower, who fled religious persecution in England in 1620 to establish a new settlement in the United States of America and who are remembered on Thanksgiving Day, the fourth Thursday in November. During the English Civil War, Independents distinguished themselves on the side of Parliament and Oliver Cromwell himself was one of them.

In the nineteenth century, Congregationalism grew significantly, becoming the largest body of Old Dissent, as opposed to the New Dissent of Methodism. The

Lea Road Church in 1908.

number of their churches rose from 229 in England and Wales in 1718 to 3,244 in 1851. The development of Congregationalism in Wolverhampton reflected this national trend. Members of the old Temple Street Meeting House formed the Congregational Church in Snow Hill in 1848/9, whilst the Queen Street Congregationalists knocked down their original building and had a new and grander church built in the two years from 1864.

This imposing place of worship with its striking entrance and elegant spire to the side was designed by Charles Bidlake, a local architect who lived at Waterloo Road and who was responsible for a number of other churches locally. Queen Street, sadly knocked down in 1970, held 1,250 worshippers. Amongst them were some of the most influential families of Wolverhampton.

At the turn of the twentieth century the minister was the Rev. H. C. Carter. He is recalled as a visionary who was active in encouraging the Queen Street Church to help the poor and run charities. This outreach into the community was matched by a desire to evangelise, spread the Good News of the Gospel, and set up missions elsewhere in Wolverhampton. These included two in the town centre, at Stafford Street and York Street, and eight satellite chapels in and around Wolverhampton at Heath Town, Wombourne, Swindon, Wallheath, Tettenhall Wood, Pattingham, and Lea Road, off the Penn Road in Penn Fields.

The Lea Road chapel began in 1902 when the Queen Street Church Meeting approved the purchase of land on the corner of Lea Road and Claremont Road for

£653 and also gave a commitment to raise funds to build a Congregational School and Chapel. Within three years that money had been raised and the building began. The foundation stone was laid by Baldwin Bantock. Twice mayor of Wolverhampton, Bantock was a prosperous businessman, noted Liberal politician and strong Non-Conformist. He became the first superintendent of Lea Road Sunday School.

The new chapel was developed by 33 members of Queen Street who lived close to Lea Road and who left the mother church. Membership of the new place of worship grew steadily, reaching 90 by the end of the second year. More spectacular was the performance of the Sunday School, which boasted 277 children and 28 officers and teachers at the end of the same period.

Youth work became a priority for Lea Road Church and it soon had its own Boys' Brigade, Girls' Brigade, football team, Band of Hope and Young People's Guild; whilst short course were also given in cookery and nursing. In addition the Church provided a lending library and from 1908 a Men's Early Morning School. This began at eight in the morning on a Sunday and lessons focused upon Bible Study, contemporary issues and New Testament Greek.

So rapidly had the Lea Road Church established itself as a major centre of the community that it was quickly apparent that it needed to be extended. Members set to raising funds with gusto. The Dorcas Sewing Group made articles for sale, bricks were sold for sixpence, and a Japanese Bazaar and entertainment was held. The total of £800 was raised, allowing the vestries and parlour to be added.

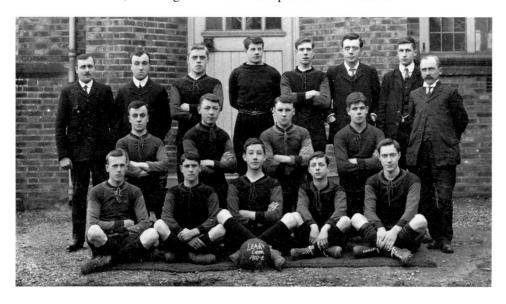

The first football team attached to Lea Road Church.

LEA RD CONGREGATIONAL C⁰ JAPANESE FAIR, 1908.

The Japanese bazaar fund raising event in 1908.

Following the First World War, Lea Road became an important place of welfare for the many local people who were suffering from the slump that followed the short post-war boom. Led by the Reverend P. A. Rose, who became minister in 1922, the Church decided to open its doors to the needy. A daily club called the Good Companions was started, and at the fireplace of the parlour those who were struggling against hard times found warmth, food and friendship.

By the mid-1920s the scale of social work at the Church was so great that it was recognised that a new sanctuary of worship was needed so that the older buildings might be freed up for work on behalf of the community. The great sum of $6,000 was required to make the dream a reality. Help was given by Queen Street and Snow Hill as well as the Staffordshire Congregational Union, but as before the members of Lea Road also threw themselves into fundraising with heart, soul and body. Through bazaars and other events they set to so as to pull in 50 thousand shillings.

At last on 7 March 1932 their efforts were rewarded when a symbolic service was held. It started in the old sanctuary, whence members processed with the Bible to the new church to give thanks. Alderman Bantock presided over the proceedings at the this the first all-electric church in Wolverhampton. During the Second World War, Lea Road Church was home to the girls of Bingley Street School and with the coming of peace, some of the women members were notable in helping returned prisoners of war, displaced persons and refugees. In the ensuing years Lea Road Church continued to be a bastion of tolerance and goodwill to all and responded positively to the changing population in Penn Fields.

By the 1960s, there was a growing number of elderly and housebound folk locally. Nellie Hutton, later Church Secretary, began to work with the Old People's Welfare Council to start a mid-day luncheon club. This later became the first Age Concern Centre in Wolverhampton. Nellie's work is highlighted today because her name was given to the Age Concern Centre in Darlington Street.

Alongside the work with the elderly, the Church began the Saints Club, a facility for youngsters who had no link with the Church. It provided social activities; an afternoon club for the young unemployed; training in skills such as woodwork; various workshops like that of child care training for young mothers, and employment training, counselling and support. The leader of the club, Chris Merrick, was awarded the MBE for her services of the young people of Penn Fields.

Many West Indian immigrants also found Lea Road Church to be a friendly and supportive place. Amongst them was Frank, whose story is in the new history of the Church. An Anglican in Jamaica, Frank began attending Lea Road in 1958 as one of the first worshippers from the Caribbean. He remembers fondly "what a warm welcome I had there; I especially remember Dora Kimberley and then dear Nellie Hupton". Frank's family all got a lot from Lea Road "and later on I was pleased to be an Elder and serve the church. It is important for me to be with my brothers and sisters in Christ."

Alderman Bantock.

Nellie Hupton, a tireless worker for the elderly.

Chris Merrick MBE with some of her 'Saints'.

In 1972 the Church voted to become part of the United Reform Church and ten years later it appointed its first Caribbean minister, the Reverend James Ryan from Saint Lucia. By the end of the 1980s, however, it was clear that the building was becoming worn and that the congregation was ageing. If the Church was to carry on its good work then it had to make a momentous decision and revitalise itself. The members took that leap of faith and authorised the demolition of the Church.

The new Church was opened in 1994. On the foundation stone a simple inscription proclaims, "Built by faith to serve God and this Community". Lea Road and its congregation do that, as they have done for 100 years. With a community worker and the Pride of Penn Fields project, a busy Junior Church, the Asian Calvary Church, and a host of groups meeting at the Church, Lea Road is a true servant both to God and the people of Penn Fields.

A cracking book called *Lea Road Church. The First 100 years. A story of vision, faith and service, 1905-2005* has been compiled by Joan Lloyd and Anne Peters. They have delved deeply into a wide range of sources to bring to the fore the history of the church and have done so devotedly and successfully. Crucially, they make it plain that important as the fabric of the church is "the real story of Lea Road does not lie in architecture, stained glass or precious items". Rather it lies in "the courage, faith and service of the many generations of Christians who have worshipped and witnessed there". The book is priced at £3 and can be obtained from the Church or by telephoning 01902 893527.

Chapter 16

SALEM AND WYRLEY BONKERS

Salem. It is a word that draws us inexorably across the Atlantic to the town of Salem in Massachusetts. In 1692 this settlement in New England was overwhelmed by the hysteria and terror of the infamous Witch Trials, during which 24 people – mostly women – were hung or died in prison. It was a terrible and violent event in a place ironically the name of which actually means peace – and it is through this the true sense of salem that we come to understand why it was given as the name of chapels across England.

Related to the Hebrew word shalom and the Arabic word salaam, salem comes to notice in the Old Testament – the source of much inspiration for the Methodists of South Staffordshire and elsewhere. In the Book of Genesis it is recounted how God told Abraham that he and his people should leave his country and go and live in Canaan. They did so, but after a time they moved on to Egypt before returning to the Promised Land. Abraham and his folk then settled in Canaan itself, whilst his nephew, Lot, and his followers dwelled in the plain of Jordan.

Unhappily the land was wracked by wars between different tribes, during one of which Lot, his group and his goods were taken captive. Abraham and his servants pursued the captors and "smote them", releasing his nephew. On the way back to Canaan, Abraham was met by Melchizedek, king of Salem, "who brought forth bread and wine; and he was the priest of the most high God. And he blessed him and said, Blessed be Abraham of the most high God, possessor of heaven and earth. And blessed be the most high God, which hath delivered thine enemies into thy hand." Abraham then gave Melchizedek a tithe, a tenth, of his booty from the victory.

Melchizedek means king of righteousness and he was the king of Salem, of peace. He is only mentioned again briefly in the Old Testament in Psalms and then several times in the Book of Hebrews in the New Testament. His identity and purpose are debated, but what is not in doubt is the importance of the word Salem. Many of the early settlers of America were Dissenters, that is they dissented from the teachings of the Church of England. For them the New World was a place of hope – hope of religious tolerance, hope of peace and hope of a better life. Deeply knowledgeable of the Bible they scoured it for names to give to their settlements and which would symbolise their hopes. Salem was one of them.

In the same way, the English Methodists of the late eighteenth and early nineteenth centuries looked for peace and a land free of religious bigotry. But unlike the Pilgrim Fathers and later Puritan emigrants to America, they did not flee England. Instead they sought to make their chapels havens of peace and symbols of charity, patience and forbearance. Salem was a most apt name to proclaim these powerful messages, not only for Methodists but also for old Dissenters such as Baptists and Congregationalists. Thus there are Salem Chapels in Wales, Lincolnshire, Devon, West Yorkshire and elsewhere, whilst in our own region there is one in Cheslyn Hay in Staffordshire.

Cheslyn Hay is as intriguing a name as Salem. In Anglo Saxon, a 'gehaeg' meant an enclosure. Over time, the 'ge' part of the word was dropped and haeg developed into hay or hey. In this case the enclosure meant a part of a forest fenced in for hunting – and, of course, Cheslyn Hay lies on Cannock Chase, that great medieval hunting ground. As for Cheslyn, it is from the Anglo Saxon cist and hlinc and signifies a coffin ledge or terrace, perhaps referring to a place where a coffin or a chest had been found.

Given as Chysteling and Cheslynhaye in documents dated between 1252 and 1290, Cheslyn Hay was rarely mentioned on its own in descriptions of Cannock Chase. In Robert Plot's *Natural History of Staffordshire* (1686) it is noted as a place where iron ore was got, whilst he also remarked that the "Plains or Hays below" Cannock Wood were in great part

John Hawkins, one of the stalwarts of the Salem in the nineteenth century. Thanks to the Museum of Cannock Chase. The photos in this chapter are taken from an excellent publication by Cheslyn Hay and District Local History Society Members Siân Alcott, Rob Allan, Dianne Ashdown, Pat Everiss, Trevor McFarlane and Dorothy Shenton. It is called History of Salem Church 1855-2005 and priced at it is available from Trevor on 01922 414772 or trevorandjan@onetel.com I commend the Society on its sterling work, its enthusiasm and its dedication to bringing to the fore the history of Chelsyn Hay. This latest book is an important addition to their publications and is an informed, thoroughly researched yet colourful and accessible history of the Salem.

"covered only with the purple odoriferous Ling." By the later eighteenth century the folk of Cheslyn Hay were well known for making besoms from this ling, or heather.

Pronounced beesums, these were brooms made by making a head from a bundle of heather. Smaller twigs were packed in the centre of the head to make a firm bed for the shaft. This was then bound tightly with hemp cane and then a ready-tapered shaft was driven and packed into the head. A strong nail was knocked into the cane binding and the sweeping end of the head was trimmed with an axe. It took a day to collect the ling; another day to make 50 or 60 besoms; and then three or more days were spent hawking the finished besoms to housewives, who swished them sideways across stone floors, back yards and paths and to farmers who used dozens of them for brushing yards and cleaning out stables, cow sheds and pig sties.

A fuller account of Cheslyn does not come until 1834 in William White's *History, Gazetteer and Directory of Staffordshire*, in which the place was described as "an extra parochial liberty, including two farms, a colliery, and the large but irregularly-built village of Wyrley Bank, which extends from 1 mile S. of Cannock, to the township of Great Wyrley, where there is a branch of the Wyrley and Essington canal, and several coal mines. It has 646 inhabitants."

Extra parochial indicated that Cheslyn Hay was outside or not part of the parish structure of the Church of England. As for liberty, this had two meanings,

Salem FC in 1922/23, including Billy Benson, Percy Hudson, Fred Smith, Reg Hawkins, Billy Baker, Harry Shorter and Brough.

A soup kitchen during the hard and hungry times of the Miners' Strike of 1926. Left to right are Mrs Hicken, Mrs Richards, Mrs Biddle, Mrs Walters, Mrs A. Perks, Mrs L. Hitchens, Mrs Gough, Irene, Murrena Hacket (the organiser), S. Leach, Mrs Windsor, Mrs Wollaston, Mrs Brown, Mrs Savage, Mrs E. Perks, Mrs Bate and young Miss Bate. Murrena Hackett and her husband, Walter, took over the butchery business of John hall in the High Street and their soup kitchen at the back of the church was invaluable for many. They also served home-made faggots and pieces to the clammed children of the village.

First it could refer to a district in which miners searched for ore and which had its own laws and customs; and second it could be a collection of manors or a sub-division of a manor from which was excluded the sheriff, the chief officer of the Crown in a county who was responsible for carrying out the law and keeping peace and good order.

Because of its relatively free status from Church and Crown - and perhaps in much the same way as The Lye - it seems that Cheslyn Hay drew to it squatters. Too often these folk are denigrated as shiftless and feckless. In reality they were poor people who scratted to make a living and who had no choice other than seek a spot on common land where the lord and other authorities could not stop them from enclosing a scrap of ground and putting up a small and humble shelter. An added appeal of living in a liberty was that squatters were free of controls from the high and mighty.

Salem School teachers in 1929. On the back row second and third from the left are W. Thomas and F. Barnett, whilst second from the right is Roland Ridgway. On the middle row F. Barnett and B. Plant are first and second on the left; and on the front row (left to right) are Bert Heminsley, Kathleen Benton, Harold Wollaston, E. Brough, Smith, Doris Smith, Herbert Dace, unknown, and Vic Kickman.

Unsurprisingly the independent character of the folk of Cheslyn Hay angered the wealthy and provoked derogatory comments. White explained that Wyrley Bank had a few good houses and "a great number of cottages in every variety of rude architecture, from the clap-built shed to the convenient dwelling, occupied chiefly by colliers and ling besom makers. Before the common was enclosed, this place, on account of its extra parochial exemption from civil authority, became the great resort of beggars and lawless vagabonds, many of whom raised mud cottages on the heath, and enclosed small plots of garden ground, which after an unmolested enjoyment of several years, they claimed as their own freehold property. It then became a nursery for illegitimate children; and wandering mendicants on being asked where they came from, commonly replied, 'from Wyrley Bank, God bless you'."

Like the free miners of the Forest of Dean in Gloucestershire, the besom (broom) makers of Wyrley Bank, or Wyrley Bonk as they called it, were unfettered by the restraints of the establishment and as such they were feared and decried. It is a pity that none of these early Wyrley Bonkers was able to leave us their own stories to counter the prejudice of the well-off who resented those of the poor who lived self-determining lives. That bigotry can be seen clearly in White's remark that "the opening of the neighbouring coal mines, however, brought some respectable inhabitants to the place", with the result "that the liberty is now nearly as civilised as its neighbours".

The besom makers are as shadowy as the history of Cheslyn Hay before the sinking of the mines locally, for it was with the arrival of the colliers that the place became better known. The miners also brought with them Methodism. Many of them hailed from the Black Country, where John Wesley's preachings had made a powerful impact and where Methodism was burgeoning amongst the working class. Moreover, because there was no Anglican parish church in Cheslyn Hay, the locality was an added attraction to Methodists.

In the early days, they met to worship in the thatched barn of Mr Gasser. It boasted a pulpit, a gallery for the congregation and an oblong window at each end. Such simple places of worship were common across Staffordshire, but as elsewhere as the number of worshippers grew then there arose a need for better and purpose-built places of worship. In Cheslyn Hay this meant that the barn was pulled down in 1806 and replaced by what became the Old Chapel.

And again as in the Black Country and other districts, the sustained expansion of Methodism in Chelsyn Hay meant that this chapel itself quickly became too small. After thirteen years it was enlarged. This was followed in 1824 by the move of the Sunday school from the Old Chapel to the new British Schoolroom at Wood's Lot in Station Street.

Before the gradual onset of a national system of schooling after the Education Act of 1870, the provision of schooling in England was patchy, piecemeal and inadequate. Middle and upper-class parents could pay for their children to be educated by governesses or at private and public schools, but many working-class families could not afford even the small fees charged by local Dame Schools, where an often elderly lady taught the rudiments of reading and writing. Into this educational gap stepped religious bodies. In order to try and an inculcate youngsters in the tenets of the Church of England, the National Society opened up many schools; whilst the Non-Conformists supported the British and Foreign Society, to which the British school in Cheslyn Hay was affiliated.

This was a day school, that is, it taught pupils Monday to Friday; but on Sundays the building was run by the Salem. Children attended both in the morning and afternoon and were taught the alphabet and writing along with Bible study and Testament classes.

Within a couple of decades it became obvious that even the expanded chapel could not cope with the needs of an active and swelling congregation and so in 1853 land adjoining the Old Chapel was purchased. A Building Committee guided the development of the new chapel. It comprised Thomas Crockett (chairman) from a family of wood staplers in Cannock; John Parry (secretary), William Crutchley; and Cornelius Whitehouse.

On 7 August 1854 hundreds of worshippers and well wishers gathered to watch Thomas Crockett lay the foundation stone. Three years later, after alterations and improvements, the Salem Chapel was opened for worship. It was part of the Methodist New Connexion, a movement which had broken away from the Wesleyan Methodists in 1797. This split had arisen over the views of Alexander Kirkham. He believed that the Methodists had to separate from the Church of England and have their own ministers. Moreover he asserted the position and rights of the ordinary members of the church. This meant that those who went with the New Connexion were part of a separate and independent sect that believed that the laity should have more power whilst the ministers had less.

As a statement from the second Conference of the Methodist New Connexion declared, "It was not from an affectation of singularity that determined us to proceed in supporting the rights and liberties of the people.... It was a conviction arising from scripture that all the members of Christ's body are one; and that the various officers of it should act by the general approbation and appointment of the people."

Despite such egalitarian thinking, numbers belonging to the Methodist New Connexion grew but slowly. Members tended to live in remote areas and as late as 1847 it boasted less than 20,000 members nationally. But it seems fitting that this democratic religious group had a stronghold in Cheslyn Hay, a place whose people had always been self-reliant, free-thinking and self-determining.

The Salem thrived and in 1880 the Reverend A. Smith was appointed as its first minister. A year later he was succeeded by the Reverend T. G. Seymour. Their tenure set the pattern for generally short but successful ministries. Then in 1889, the Old Chapel itself was knocked down and replaced by the present Sunday school; and nine years afterwards the Salem was made bigger, making the beautiful chapel that remains a vital part of the whole life of Cheslyn Hay.

Befitting a religious body that valued highly the members of the congregation, the significance of the Salem to Cheslyn Hay was enhanced by a number of godly and good-hearted individuals. Amongst them was Joseph Hawkins. He laid one of the four memorial tablets in the wall of the new Sunday school. Originally a blacksmith, through dint of hard work, determination and application, Joseph became the owner of the Coppice Colliery and a respected engineer. Indeed, George Stephenson, the railroad pioneer, consulted Joseph about mine drainage.

Joseph and his wife had four sons: John, Edward, Henry and Thomas. All were devoted church workers; whilst according to the fascinating new history of the Salem, Henry's wife, Sarah Jane, was "a great spiritual force in the church which she visited every day. Her enthusiasm lighted the holy flame in other hearts and she was known and honoured by all the ministers." The Hawkins bond with the Salem reached deep into the twentieth century with Arnold and Albert, cousins who were both fine organists and resolute workers for the church.

Another leading figure in the early history of the Salem was Samuel Whitehouse. His grandson, Cornelius, founded the edge tool firm of C. Whitehouse and Sons, but he was also a musician of note who composed Christmas Carols and popular music for church services.

Like Cornelius, William Crutchley was one of the four men who were on the Building Committee of the new chapel, and he has been praised as "the spiritual leader of the church and a great power for the good of the village, filling every church office for sixty-six years". A prominent lay preacher, William was married to Mary and at their home they had a Prophets' Chamber, a room reserved especially for the visiting ministers in which to rest. It was well needed. The Reverend Samuel Hulme, for example, used to walk sixteen miles from Birmingham to preach at Cheslyn Hay, after which he would walk a further twelve miles to Stafford.

A noteworthy local preacher was James Lawson. He also copied the original Salem Baptism Register from 1790 to 1821, to which he added captivating remarks. Amongst other matters, these detailed that Joe Baker was a prominent cock fighter, that Gideon Ousley moved to Ireland and that William Whitehouse sadly lost a leg after he teased Fisher's goat on the Sabbath and was then butted fiercely by the animal.

The annual Sunday School Rose Queen float.

James preached his last sermon at the Salem with his face bandaged up. When he had finished he told the congregation that the doctor has informed him that he was suffering from cancer and had only three months left to live. Standing tall and dignified, he proclaimed, "I am now ready to be offered up and the time of my departure is at hand. I have fought the good fight. I have finished the course. I have kept the faith."

Three months later James died. His faith was inspirational. It was and is shared by so many others associated with the Salem. This faith is not inward-looking and exclusive, rather it reaches out and embraces all, so that the Salem has become more than an important place of worship it has become a crucial element in the life of all the people of Cheslyn Hay and Wyrley Bank, irrespective of class or creed. Its societies, clubs and guilds have been – and many still are – essential to the well being of the community. That the Salem has continued to be a beacon of faith and active citizenship is a testament to the devotion and Christian charity of its founders and early members.

Chapter 17

A CIVIC FAMILY: THE FULLWOODS

What a thrill it must have been to have been there in the late 1800s at the start of a transport revolution that would transform society as radically as it would change the means of travel. Those pioneers of the automotive industry dreamt heady dreams of giving people the freedom to move about the land in a quicker, cheaper and more comfortable way compared to horse-driven vehicles. Their wonderful new concept was that of the horseless carriage. Driven forward personal ambition, mechanical skill, scientific yearning, and the inquisitiveness of the eager mind, these men had wide visions but yet not even they could have imagined the massive impact that their invention of the motor car would have on the lives of each person in the most powerful nations in the world.

Within a few years of the trailblazing experiments of the innovative few, great factories had spring up in Britain, Germany, France, Italy and the United States – factories that not only made cars but also produced the parts for them. Tens of thousands of people worked in these mighty manufactories in cities such as Detroit in America and Birmingham and Coventry in England. All three claimed with pride and some boastfulness the title of motor city – but there was another town that had been close to joining them and which too made its mark upon the early automobile trade. That town was Wolverhampton.

The idea of motorised transport had effectively originated in Germany in 1885 when Gottlieb Daimler had fitted one of his engines to a bicycle and gave rise to the idea of the motorcycle. The next year Karl Benz ran his first motor vehicle on the road and so began the age of the car. These German groundbreakers influenced a number of Britons and in 1890 Frederick Simms acquired the rights for Daimler's engine patents both in the United Kingdom and its empire. In turn, these patents were sold on and as a result in December 1896, the Daimler Motor Company was registered.

Yet there were also, although British, mechanics who seem to have developed independently their own thoughts and practices. They included Frederick Lanchester and Herbert Austin. Born and raised in London, Lanchester came to Birmingham in 1888. Seven years later, in Taylor Street, Nechells, he created the first four-wheel car which was petrol driven and was all British. First driven on the road early in 1896, this vehicle was the 5bhp Stanhope Phaeton and, like all other early motor cars, it looked like a carriage that could have been drawn by horses. Crucially, this vehicle was the first anywhere designed to run on tyres filled with air. These tyres were hand made by Dunlop, then based in Dublin but soon to move to Aston Cross, Birmingham. Three years later, in 1899, the Lanchester Engine Company of Birmingham was registered.

As for Herbert Austin, he was a farm bailiff's son who was raised in Yorkshire, but as he stressed later, "strangely enough, even in my very early years it was for things mechanical I had the greatest love". Fascinated by geometrical drawings, Austin developed a keen eye for size and proportions. At the same time, he was deeply attracted to the music of the great composers and to works of art and for the rest of his life his passion for the mechanical was infused with an urge to make things that were artistic. After leaving school, Austin joined his uncle in Australia and became an apprentice at Longland's Foundry Company, where he received 'a thorough training as a mechanic' and took out his first patent - for a locking plate for a railway fish-plate bolts.

After his apprenticeship, Austin became the manager of a small engineering business which carried out work for an Australian firm, the Wolseley Sheep Shearing Machine Company. Rising to manager of the Wolseley, Austin began to travel Australia. Talking to sheep farmers he recognised the vital need for reliable equipment for those who were distant from suppliers and swift repairs – and also the need for a good and fast means of movement. He later emphasised that it was in the isolated places the Outback "that I made a kind of compact with myself that I would one day, by some means or other, build motor cars that could be used by these lonely yet loveable people of the bush".

His opportunity came with the relocation of the Wolseley to Birmingham. Perhaps affected by a visit to Paris, where he had examined the "very crude internal combustion engines that were in existence at the time", he built a tri-car which had two wheels at the front and one at the back. Finished in 1895 at his home, swiftly he took it out on the Coventry Road. The next year the budding car maker persuaded the board of the Wolseley to support his automobile venture and in 1896 he produced the Wolseley Autocar Number 1. This had two wheels at the rear and one to the front, and a year later it was followed by another three-wheeler. It was this vehicle that Austin ran to Rhyl and back in 1898. He averaged a speed of 8 mph, carried two passengers and had no breakdown on the 250-mile plus trip. Increasingly drawn to starting up his own business, at last Austin struck out for himself in 1905 and set up a new company in Longbridge.

For all the importance of Lanchester and Austin it would be unwise to neglect the car-making pioneers of Wolverhampton. Prominent amongst them was Thomas Hugh Parker, son of the founder of the Electric Construction Company. He is brought to the fore in a wonderful website belonging to the Wolverhampton History

& Heritage Society www.localhistory.scit.wlv.ac.uk. There can be few local websites in the country that are as wide-ranging, informed, interesting and illuminating as this one. Embracing deeply-researched articles and as deeply-researched sections on buildings, people and industries, it is a boon to anyone wishing to find out more about one of the most important places in the kingdom.

Praised as "a brilliant innovator and inventor", Parker showed an early interest in powered vehicles and claimed to have had a battery powered car running as early as 1884. This was followed by several other cars, whilst Thomas is also credited with the design and manufacture of E.C.C.'s famous 'electric dog-cart', which was built in 1896 and was steered by reins. Some of Parker's cars included modern features such as hydraulic brakes on all four wheels and four wheel steering, and he claimed to have invented the spark plug, the monoblock engine and the carburettor.

Despite Parker's inventiveness, the E.C.C. never produced cars commercially – unlike Sunbeam, which was founded by John Marston. Hailing from Shropshire, Marston came to Wolverhampton to become an apprentice as a japanner and tinsmith. Like Austin, Marston made himself and through hard graft, determination and perseverance he became one of the largest japanners in Wolverhampton. And also like Austin, he was keen on new modes of transport – but in his case it was the bicycle. The tale goes that Marston was a keen cyclist but that he had problems riding because of his short frame. Consequently, his works foreman, William Newill, built a special cycle with a low frame. It was splendidly finished – as a japanner would have done - in black and gold leaf. John's wife, Ellen, supposedly saw the sun reflected in the high gloss finish and so the bicycle was called 'The Sunbeam'. It was registered in 1888 and bicycle production began.

Eleven years later Marston began to experiment with making cars and in 1901 he produced the Sunbeam-Mabley. The metal ware and japanning part of the business was then sold and Marston's focus became the making of bicycles and cars. In March 1905 the Sunbeam Motor Car Co. Ltd was formed at the Moorfield Works, off Villiers Street, and within a few years the manufacture of motorbikes had also begun.

Edward Lisle was another ingenious Wulfrunian who moved into car making through bicycle production at his Star works in Stewart Street. In about 1897 he dismantled a Benz vehicle, converted its measurements from metric to imperial, and incorporated a number of other changes and improvements. Henceforth Star would become associated with motorcars and not bicycles.

Parker, Marston and Lisle were not on their own. There were other important local contributors to the growth of the car industry, like Harry Stevens who developed engines for cars and motorbikes. At the same time car production was the catalyst for the growth of businesses vital to the running of an automobile. One such was the Staffordshire Tyre Company.

For generations Wolverhampton has been associated with tyres through the massive Goodyear plant. Established in 1927 on the edge of the town at site of the disused enamellers, Macfarlaine and Robinson, it became a major feature of Wolverhampton. Yet tyres were important locally for many years before that and the Staffordshire Tyre Company remained a key business until it was actually taken over by Goodyear.

Important for their input into the development of the wider car industry in the West Midlands, the Fullwoods are also significant because they exhibit two crucial aspects of successful business families in the early twentieth century. First they adhered to the belief in public service. Never able to match the Manders for either wealth or influence, still the Fullwoods played no mean part in the public life of Wolverhampton. Secondly, they exhibit the qualities of adaptability and vision that were so vital to the emergence of the West Midlands as one of the greatest manufacturing regions that the world has ever known.

The Fullwoods trace their descent to a James who died in the terrible cholera epidemic that ravaged Bilston in 1832. Out of a population of just under 15,000, a total

Sitting are Ann and James Treen Fullwood with their children before he set up in business in 1908.

Queen Square with new business of James Treen Fullwood circled.

of 752 men, women and children were killed. The town was devastated by the loss of so many lives in such a short time. James himself was a tinman aged 39 who had lived at Brook Street, New Town. He died on 27 August and was buried with more than 300 other poor souls in the graveyard of Swan Bank Wesleyan Methodist Church.

James left at least one son, also called James. He was born just a few months before his father was to die and must have had a tough upbringing, but like so many working folk, he had neither the time nor the energy to leave behind his life story. Moving from Bilston to Wolverhampton at some stage in his life, it seems that James must have worked hard and reached a more comfortable working-class lifestyle, for his second son, James Treen, was able to become a pupil teacher in 1881 when he was sixteen. He was amongst the first generation of English youngsters, other than the rich, who had received a proper education. The fact that he was not taken out of school at the age of ten or eleven to work in a factory or mine meant that his father must have been able afford for James Treen to stay on in his education.

The position of pupil teacher was an important one and youngsters who were barely into their mid teens became responsible for large classes. Importantly the job was also a route into the lower middle class – a route of which James Treen took full advantage. By 1892 he was a hardware clerk married to Ann Blenkin. Such a job was not well paid, and it would appear that James Treen was keen to use his hands as well as his mind, for at some point he began working on tyre repairs and retreading. What made him move in that direction is not known, but just as John Marston was struck by the cycle craze of the late nineteenth century so must have been James Treen.

Saving successfully, in 1908 and at the age of 43 he made an adventurous move and bought a business. It was not the usual thing that a middle-aged man with a family would do, but impelled by the need to become his own gaffer James Treen placed his future in his own control. The business that he acquired was a tyre vulcanising business called the Staffordshire Motor Tyre Repairing Co. It cost £100, a sum that was the equivalent of a year's wages for a highly skilled man or a clerk, and it was situated in a prominent location in Queens Square, Wolverhampton.

In 1913, following a move to new premises at Chapel Ash, the business became the Staffordshire Motor Tyre Co. Ltd. By now James Treen had been joined by his second oldest son, Harold. According to an article in the *Goodyear News* in 1958 there was little time for leisure, "with each working week then lasting the full 7-days round, and much night as well as day repair work being handled in the process of building up".

Harold's older brother, Frederick, was not involved in the business. His grandson, David, recites that "family legend states Fred didn't get along too well with his father. This culminated in an incident with a box of matches, a living room gas mantle and

The Staffordshire Tyre Company in Chapel Ash in 1958.

an explosion at the family home in Mander Street which resulted in an injury to his father". According to the 1901 Census, nine-year old Fred was living with his grandfather in Bristol Street, Wolverhampton. Later he went on to become a carpenter and establish an ironmonger's shop in Newhampton Road West. He passed this on to his son, Anthony.

During the First World War, James Treen had to cope with the expanding business on his own. The Government directed labour either into the Armed Forces or into important war work and young Harold was moved into engineering. His brother Harry went into aircraft repair work, whilst another brother, Harry, saw four years active service in the Army.

In 1919 and with the coming of peace, "the Fullwood family came together again as one redoubtable working unit and, for a number of years, father, three sons and two daughters worked together in re-establishing their pre-war sales and service organisation and in consolidating and extending their post-war activities". In this period

The Mayor of Wolverhampton, Alderman Harold Fullwood, attending a Remembrance Service at St Peter's Church.

the family adopted the catch slogan 'See Fullwood First' and supplied tyres to both Guy Motors, the major Wolverhampton commercial vehicle manufacturer, and the Sunbeam – which recognised the close ties between the two companies in a special way. The Sunbeam directors presented James Treen Fullwood with a replica model of the 1,000 hp Sunbeam 'slug' that was driven by Major Segrave in 1927 in American and which broke the land speed record by reaching almost 204 miles per hour. This miniature was one of only eleven that were made.

Despite the Depression of the 1930s, the Staffordshire Tyre Co. was expanding and it extended its operations by opening the Shropshire Tyre Company Ltd in

Shrewsbury. With Jim Fullwood as managing director, this new venture soon encompassed new branches in Oakengates, Welshpool and Whitchurch. Harry Fullwood also had his own responsibilities, as in 1931 Modern Tyres Service (Walsall) Ltd was started.

The Mayor of Wolverhampton, Alderman Edward Yardley Fullwood, being prepared for his inauguration in 1967.

After the death of James Treen Fullwood in 1939, the overall management of the companies passed to Harold Fullwood, who remained at Chapel Ash where his son Jim was sales manager, and his other, Ted, was service manager. The *Goodyear News* declared in 1958 that "these premises constitute one of the finest tyre service stations to be found anywhere in the world, where any tyre, from the smallest wheelbarrow to the largest earthmover, can be supplied or serviced". Indeed, following an extension for storage in 1951, "the total floor area used for repairs, sales and service is upwards of 20,000 square feet".

A man of clear engineering aptitude, Harold is reputed to have been the designer of the first traffic light installation in the United Kingdom in Princess Square, Wolverhampton; and he is said to have also designed an automatic traffic light system for Oxford Street in London. His business success was matched by his success in the public life of Wolverhampton. An alderman and mayor in 1952/3, he lived at The Grove, a large property off Wood Road, Tettenhall. During the Second World War, a German bomber looking for the nearby aircraft factory of Boulton Paul, had dropped its bombs by mistake on the house. Harold then bought it and restored it. His son, Edward, followed him in to public life and also received the honour of the mayorship of Wolverhampton in 1967/8.

A few years later, the Staffordshire Tyre Company came to an end as an independent presence and was bought out by Goodyear; but in the Fullwoods and their impact both on the economic and civic affairs of Wolverhampton, we catch sight of one of the many middling sort of families whose work and activities were vital for the wellbeing of our towns.

There is a website on the Fullwood family put together by David Fullwood www.fullwood.org.uk. I thank David for his generosity in allowing me to access his family archive to write this chapter.